Enarchae

JN097070

Stean Anthony

Yamaguchi Shoten, Kyoto

山口書店，京都

Transliterated Greek words in the title are from the beginning of the Book of Genesis

1.1. ἐν ἀρχῇ ἐποίησεν ὁ θεὸς τὸν οὐρανὸν καὶ τὴν γῆν. (LXX)

Image on the cover of the book

"Sailing Over the Caribbean From the International Space Station." Portions of Cuba, the Bahamas and the Turks and Caicos Islands are viewed from the International Space Station, as the orbital complex flew 252 miles above the Atlantic Ocean. At left is the aft end of the Progress 70 resupply ship from Russia attached to the station's Pirs docking compartment.

Image Credit: NASA   Last Updated: Jan. 31, 2019   Editor: Yvette Smith

See website: Astronomy Picture of the Day Archive   Nasa

https://apod.nasa.gov/apod/archivepix.html

Stean Anthony thanks NASA for the use of this image.

Enarchae

© 2021 Stean Anthony
Author's profits
See end of book for details
PRINTED IN JAPAN

FOR JERUSALEM

Keter	crown
Chochmah	wisdom
Binah	understanding
Daat	knowledge
Chesed	kindness
Gevurah	strength
Tiferet	beauty
Netzach	victory
Hod	splendor
Yesod	foundation
Malchut	kingship

Enarchae

Contents

Episode Number & Title

119. Saint Legends
120. Nablus Soap Factory
121. To Learn & Enrich
122. Al-Kebir Mosque
123. Voice Tender
124. Watchers
125. Nablus Baklava
126. Hammam Al Shifa
127. Shiloh
128. Hannah
129. Beitel
130. Taybeh Lager
131. Taybeh Festival
132. Festival Takoyaki
133. Increase Festivals
134. The Taybeen
135. Palestinian House
136. Struggling On
137. George & Dragon
138. Fireball
139. Birzeit Garden
140. Anani
141. Tree Icons
142. Palestinian Dress
143. Harris Thawb
144. Wall of Faces
145. Holy Soap
146. Pipes Wailing
147. Peace Casino
148. Basketball
149. Shawarma

10

Acknowledgement
I have benefited from information from Chabad.org website
and other websites. Thank you.

For episode 243 see text of sermon given by Martin Luther
King on Easter Day 1959 published on website of The
Martin Luther King, Jr. Research and Education Institute,
Stanford University.

Information in this book comes from various sources. The
book is fictional, and the characters fictional. The purpose is
educational, and the point of view is that of the author alone
and does not represent an official point of view of church or
institution.

Preface

This is a serialized novel in the form of a calendar. The central character is Phim, who appeared in *Exnihil* (Book 1 in this series) and *Bərešitbara* (Book 2). *Enarchae* is Book 3. Phim also appears in my earlier novel, *Mosaic Angel* (still unfinished). There is a paragraph of prose per day. Snapshots of story, poetic phrases.

Powerful propeller on the nose, two large floats under the wings. They had been painted white with stars, crosses and crescents. The floats struck the canvas awning and neatly ripped it off. The seaplane lifted, thundering upon them and circled around for another attack.   Ange said, Watch out. They might drop something.   The window behind the wing had opened. As it passed over, an arm pushed out a small package. It struck the deck near Phim. Sal grabbed it and threw it in the water. A mighty explosion rocked the boat. It circled again.

Jo shouted, Use the net.   No time. The arm pushed out another package. Small homemade bomb. Little brown parcel. Plastic explosive. At the front of the boat Yaeli caught it, and hurled it away.   Hit the deck, shouted Sal, and hold on. Another massive explosion, and the boat rocked violently. A great wave washed over.   Sal and Ange grabbed the net, and tied the rope to the wheel-pillar. As the plane came low, using poles, they caught the net on the floats. The package went out. It fell in the trailing net. The net pulled tight. The wheel-pillar held.

Kaboom! Just as the seaplane plunged into the lake, the bomb in the net beneath it exploded, breaking the body of the plane neatly in two. Three men in the water. Phim recognized one of the faces from earlier when they had shone the lights. Wizened reptilian. They shouted, Ah! Ah! Burning! Lake Galilee water was burning them. Phim said, Throw them a ring. Reluctantly, Ange threw it to them. They pulled them out and tied them up. Not a word was spoken to them. Their faces were fury. One hissed at Phim, We would destroy thee. We hate thee.

A launch came racing towards them
from Tiberias. There was a helicopter in
the air above them. They were escorted
back to Tiberias, and salvage operations
were started on the broken plane, held
up by its floats. After questioning and
taking details, the three men were taken
into custody, and they were free to go.
Let's stay close to the lake for a few days,
said Yaeli.   Irma said, Let's pray
together for the lake.   Phim said, There
was damage.   Ange said, This is a holy
place.   They stood by the shore as the
sun set behind them, and prayed.

As they walked back to Tiberias, Sal said, A reservoir of fresh water in a dry land. In late summer the water is warm and tastes of algae, after the winter rains it's cold and sweet. There were battlefields. The Aramean kings threatened Israel at the time of David (1000 BCE). The Horns of Hattin (1187 CE). Allenby and Lawrence took Palestine with Arab and Anzac cavalry (1918). The Roman Empire was also here, said Yaeli, drily. Have we at last entered the time of peace? Phim said, I think it will depend on us.

They parked outside the Scots Hotel, and booked in. Let's rest for an hour and then try the hotel sauna and pools, said Sal. It was a former hospital which had been turned into a deluxe resort. Just what I need, said Phim. Phim and Sal walked to the men's section. See you later, said Irma and Yaeli. They changed into the gowns. Togas, said Phim. After a shower they lay face down on the bed. Phim on the left, Sal on the right. Two very muscular men with oiled torsos appeared. Oh, thought Phim.

Turkish massage, said one of the men. Sal said, This should be memorable. Phim fought a surge of anxiety. The two men got to work. Pushing, pulling, and pummeling the muscles. Aah, said Phim. They were expert. A world of stress and misery began to collapse. Sal said, It hurts, but it's good. One of the men said, Where are you from? They chatted. They were qualified Turkish masseurs from Ankara. You'll be walking on air after this, he said. It removes poisons. Phim could not speak. A grief came, seeing his mother. He fought a strange urge to weep.

8   Jan 8   Pay Up

As they sipped a Tio Pepe in the hotel lounge, Phim listened to the guests who stood by the bar. One was attractive. Glossy dark brown hair, large dark eyes, full curvy figure. They were speaking Hebrew. Phim thought about her. On the waterslide together in Tiberias. All of sudden a man stood beside him, saying, That'll be 100 shekels. I'll take drachmas. I want them authentically dated older than 2000 years. He was wearing a white coat, like a pharmacist. I can't pay, thought Phim. Anxiety seized the pit of the stomach.   Pay up or prison, said the man.

But I don't have any shekels or drachmas, said Phim. What are these then, said the man, reaching deep into Phim's left shoulder and pulling out a handful. These will do. But Phim felt diminished, unable to grab hold of what was happening, something had been lost. I cannot pay with that, he cried, I will not live. Then, the man sneered at him, you will have to get someone to help you, because I will take the rest, and you can sleep, good riddance to you, worthless trash. Phim found himself sitting in the armchair. His hand shook.

There are two ages in human history, said Yaeli. The age of low intelligence and the age of high intelligence. In the age of low intelligence, for millennia, men were in command. All positions of authority were held by men. Human society was unjust. The relation with the neighboring tribe was war. Criminals were put to death for trivial offences. In the age of high intelligence, human relations were peaceful. Resources were protected. Society was compassionate and just. Over half the positions of authority were held by women. Now tell me this. When did the age of high intelligence begin?

The tomb of a holy righteous man, said Yaeli.   His wife agreed to marry him on condition that he learnt the Torah, even though he was already forty years old. Day and night he studied and became one of the greatest rabbis. Legend ascribes him 24,000 students. He became the spirit of resistance under the Roman onslaught. The Jewish faith changed from being Temple-centred to a rabbinical faith of teacher and Book. In that turmoil we also were born, said Irma.   They admired the view, the light-blue waters of the lake were tranquil under a light-blue sky.

Rabbi Akiva 1st century executed by Romans after Bar Kokhba Revolt.

Yaeli said, It was after the Bar Kokhba revolt (132-6). Akiva was imprisoned for publicly teaching Torah, forbidden by the Romans. The Jerusalem Talmud relates that when he stood before the Roman judge, he knew that the time to recite the Shema prayer (also forbidden) had come. He recited it with a smile. The judge asked him why he was smiling. Akiva replied that all his life he had read the verse, "And you shall love your God with all your heart, with all your soul, and with all your strength," but had never been able to fulfill it.

Adapted from My Jewish Learning   https://www.myjewishlearning.com/article/rabbi-akiba/

13   Jan 13   Explain Rambam

Visiting Maimonides (Rambam's) tomb, Yaeli said, Father would pause when he was teaching us at home. He would knit his brow and say, Rabbi Moshe, why do you have to make it so hard? He would slowly reread Rambam's puzzling words. I was too young to understand, but I learnt the wonder of it. Father spoke to him as though he were there.   Mummy, Daddy can't explain Rambam.   She'd say, In a minute he will. When you grow up, you can help. Remember. Keep learning.   That was my first meeting with Maimonides, and I've been reading him all my life.

Inspired by a story told by Joseph Dov Soloveitchik (1903-1993).

Yaeli said, When the Berber Almohades swept into Islamic Cordoba (1148), safety for the Jews, who had prospered there for generations, disappeared. Maimonides and his family fled, moving to Fez in North Africa, and ending up in Cairo. Jews were welcome, and Rambam could teach and write. He became community leader (Nagid). Renowned from his youth, he produced masterly syntheses of former opinions, providing an authoritative guide to the Mishnah and Torah that is still used today. He even worked as court doctor. He was a true polymath genius. His introduction to the Mishnah "Sanhedrin" contains his famous thirteen principles.

Yaeli said, Rambam's 13 principles are used today in prayer and liturgy. They represent a core statement of the Jewish faith. We must believe in: 1 the Creator, the perfect primary cause; 2 God's unity; 3 his non-corporeality, unaffected by physical things; 4 his eternity, the first and last; 5 we must worship him alone; 6 the prophets speak truth; 7 Moses is our teacher; 8 Torah was divinely given to Moses; 9 Torah is immutable; 10 God is omniscient; 11 with God there is reward and retribution; 12 the Messiah will come; 13 the dead will be raised.

Yaeli said, Rambam, in a famous passage, shows that faith turns on the acceptance or rejection of Aristotle or Plato. Aristotle believes in the eternity of the universe (eternal substance always existed i.e. no creation by God from nothing); Plato talks about the transience of the heavens: God, who has no corporeality (being unlimited by form or time) created everything: there was a beginning; there will be an end. The first miracle was the greatest miracle; all other miracles are possible. Where then does God exist? Why did he choose whom or what he chose? Who will answer?

Inspired by Maimonides, Guide to the Perplexed Book 2 chap. 25-26.

Hush, said Yaeli.   A Rabbi was praying out aloud in English. He wore a black Homburg and was dressed as a Hassid. He chanted with uplifted voice.   His life (Moshe Chaim Luzzatto) was devoted to bringing truth and Kabbalah to the world. He was totally connected to Hashem. His merit be with us and all Israel now. May Hashem open in us allness, to express who we are, to be our true selves, to speak with full consciousness, with emotion, to know what we say, to see the consequences and meanings, amen.   Yaeli explained quietly, Hashem means "Name" (i.e. G-d).

Adapted from videoclip "Rabbi Yitzchak Schwartz, Visiting The Ramhal's Tomb,

Kabbalah Me Documentary."

18   Jan 18   Thrashing

The Rabbi concluded his prayer, and looked upwards, his face suffused with emotion. His group moved away. At the entrance to the tomb an unkempt old man in once-white robes appeared. Sunken cheeks, scruffy grey beard, fiery eyes. He had with him a white stick, about a metre and a half long. He looked at Phim, and shouted in broken English, You persist in fraud and fakery. When will you turn to me? He dashed forward and started thrashing Phim on the buttocks. Round and round the tomb they ran, Phim shouting, Ow! Ow! Please stop that!

Ange stepped smartly between and restrained the old man, but he slipped from him, and stood again at the entrance, glaring. Maggid, said Phim, not knowing why. The old man looked at him, displaying a full set of brown teeth. Ignorant insects, he shouted, and ran off. Phim said, Thank you, Ange, his buttocks stinging from the cane. Yaeli was showing the strain of suppressed hilarity. She said, Elijah, who never died, gives his spirit to the truly good. Like John the Baptist, said Joseph. Are you OK, Phim, asked Irma. My goodness, that man smelt awful.

Phim said, I always thought there was a message in Magdala but never knew what. Mary Magdalene is special to the Lord. She's given the honor of meeting him in the resurrection (John 20). She knows it's him when he speaks her name. We have heaven in Mother Mary. Magdalene was earthly but Jesus is telling us that she's very good. Was she a half-Greek?   How about Migdal, said Yaeli.   They were in the new sanctuary. An altar shaped like a boat with Lake Galilee visible in the large window. The priest lifted up the bread.

It was a mummy of a boat, held in a cradle of a thousand steel hands. Dark brown wood had slept in the mud for 2,000 years. Phim peered at it, and felt an urge to clamber aboard. Got the end there, Peter? One two fling the net. Haul her up. John stop slacking for goodness sake. Nothing? Phim, will you stop singing, you're scaring the fish away. It's you Peter. You stink like a dried carp. They don't like it. They're sensitive. Dive in and wash. Ask him if you like. Is he asleep? Again? Wake him up.

Phim had rung the sisters and asked permission to attend an early morning service in the Church, and they'd agreed. They parked outside the gate. Dawn above the eastern hills. A Franciscan sister opened the gate. To the church. A brother led the early morning Eucharist. One of the sisters was preaching. It was a good sermon. The Beatitudes, she said, describe the personality of two people. Jesus and Mary. They are clever and sublime verses, repeating the same message. Luke has four verses. Matthew eight. The difference is instructive. What's the most important? Peace-making? Is that Jesus or Mary?

Franciscan Sisters of the Immaculate Heart of Mary.

Join us for breakfast, Phim, said the sister. They walked over to the garden. It's lovely weather. In your honor, let us eat outside in the garden. Two sisters brought jugs of warm milk, espresso, biscotti, a basket of hot brioche, fruit. Phim's heart rejoiced. It was a heavenly place. Tall palm trees above well-kept lawns. Flowers. There was Lake Galilee below. A gentle breeze. Can I say a prayer, asked Phim. Blessed is God who gives us life, Blessed be this place, thank you God, amen. The brother said grace. Phim looked around and felt happy.

The guide said, The Via Maris, the main north-south trunk road ran past the town, heading southwest to the coast. The name Caphar Naum means village of comfort or compassion. Constant traffic on the road. A welcome stopover. Water the mules. Cheap fish. They were Romans, or under Roman government. Don't say any more, said Phim, we found out about that in Tunisia. The point is that Jesus Christ chose such a place for mission. Yaeli said, The strongest pillar in your house. Compassion, said Irma. For the women mostly, said Phim, and they were not Jews.

The guide continued. A prosperous town. The traffic brought trade. The Romans had a custom post where Matthew worked. What was he taxing? Roman cohorts were stationed here. Jesus healed the Centurion's servant. It might have been here that the Centurion gave money to build a synagogue. Was he a friend of Jews? Ah, said Yaeli, there you have it. Your Gospel points to the future. The "Romans" turn into new-jews (Christians), and they don't like old-Jews. They will force us to leave. You can see it in the pagan decorations put into the synagogues that they turn into churches.

Sitting in the gardens close to the Greek church. There were two tourists sharing a sandwich. Phim admired their hair, long dark glossy curls cascading over their shoulders. Where are you from, he asked. Antioch, they said. Turkish? Actually we're Syrian. Christians. A pilgrimage. A holy place, said Phim. Yes, they said. My name's Phim. They walked down to the lake. Maybe he walked on water over there, said one of the girls. It was afternoon, and very peaceful. The sunlight shimmered on the water surface. Join us for supper, if you like. They said OK.

The Syrian girls were singing. It's a song we composed about our ancestors. It's said in our family that long ago we were taken from Galilee. Slaves at first, later we became farmers in the north. The Greeks came and then Romans. We became Christian. Islam rose but we remained Christian. We still have our old language. Aramaic. It's like Arabic. What are the words of the song, asked Phim.   A long journey but God will not leave us. He walks with us all the way. His love is sure.   Beautiful, said Yaeli. Teach us the words, said Irma.

They were standing in the hexagonal church raised above the ruins of Peter's house, which could be seen through a glass floor. It's not Peter's house, said Joseph, it's Simon's. He's not called Peter until later in the Gospel of Mark. Does that matter? asked Phim. His mother-in-law has a fever. Jesus cures her. Simon is a priestly name, though Peter is a fisherman. Hebrew name. Greek name. The mother of the one he's married to is burning. Jesus cools her. Is she burning with zeal, or anger, or wickedness? Is she a pagan? There's a message, isn't there?

Mark 1.29-31; 3.16.

This must be the most important synagogue in the whole world, said Sal. Yaeli laughed. Phim said, It must be if Jesus preached here. Healing the possessed. The bread of life sermon. Sal said, We stand in a place we can share. Irma said, Do you feel anything here, Phim? Phim stood and listened, and thought. Time passed. The sound of water. A voice singing Hebrew. It sounds wonderful. Someone is explaining. A warm voice. Good to hear. I am strengthened. I feel better. I feel happy. I must learn Hebrew! Yaeli said, It might have been Aramaic.

Yaeli said, Jesus the healer, Jesus the teacher is here because he gives the comfort of the Father.   Sal said, It's the mercy of God.   It's a good place to get married, said Irma.   Phim said, Would Jesus bless young couples in love? Even before marriage?   Joseph said, We don't teach our children to have sex before marriage, but of course that was the beginning of the whole thing.   Yaeli said, Jesus is holy and wise. He looks deeper than ordinary shallow morality. He looks at the heart. Is love there?

My favorite passage, said Irma. Peter says to Jesus, You have the words of eternal life.   Yaeli said, He certainly does but I can't agree with what he said before (Jn 6.58).   Phim said, Surely the ancestors rest in God. They're alive. We must also live in God. The bread gives life.   Sal said, Live by love for one another.   There was a demonstration of how the paralytic was lowered through the roof.   There's the message. They seek compassion, said Ange. That's how all of us have improved, and must continue. We have changed and must change more.

Why all this healing and healing going on in Capharnaum? Is everybody sick? asked Phim. Joseph said, When you check the references, it becomes clear. Jesus the physician is sent to make them well. It's Isaiah, the best message about God. The truth of God. Give it to the whole world. It's time. Clean up the bad world. Here we are, a perfect place for mission. The right kind of zeal. Paul, the road, over there is Damascus. It will take a long time, but the goal is freedom for slaves. But they reject him, after all he does.

This was once an extensive wetland, but now there's only a small lake, said Phim, reading from the guidebook. The same universal story. Drain the wetlands. Cut down forests. They stood and gazed to the north. Mount Hermon had a cape of snow.   It says that there are still millions of birds passing through on their way to Africa but nowhere for them to refuel. They follow the Jordan and Nile, pointing due south. Fresh water they need, and food. But where can they find food here?   Sal said, We should be treating these places as holy and inviolable.

They were in the Reserve centre, watching a film about the pelican. It was a highly endangered species, requiring a world-habitat that was almost gone, migrating through fishless lands. They supplied 40 tons of fish in one of the pools, and thousands of pelicans were able to survive and continue to Africa. Is that what we have to do? asked Phim. It turned out that the former wetland had been absolutely vital.   On the screen, the pelican flew on powerful wings, the long beak and pouch into the wind.   How   ungainly!   How improbable! How beautiful you are, thought Phim.

What are we trying to do? asked Sal. What do you mean? said Phim. Thinking as a species, what are we trying to do? What's the purpose of all this activity? Our children are now as numerous as grains of sand. Was that our purpose?   Yaeli said, Isaiah and the Psalms give the answer.   But is destroying the natural environment the way to praise and thank God, asked Sal. Our science controls and predicts most natural events. But the garden of beauty is lost. Key species are lost. Surely God must be green.

They parked the Cruiser and strolled about. There was a dairy selling goat's cheese. Phim stared through the window. They were offering free samples. As he was about to suggest a tasting session, from one of the streets came a high-pitched roar. A white Corvette accelerated toward them. Watch out, shouted Ange. Phim, not paying attention, jumped backwards, just as the car swerved towards him. He was lifted up onto the bonnet and rolled onto the windscreen. His polo shirt rode up, and his belly button bonded with the glass. And there he stayed, stuck like glue.

The Corvette (Chevrolet Stingray) continued to accelerate, unable to see anything except Phim's belly button. Phim had examined it that morning. Black and grimy with decayed skin. He usually cleaned it with a toothbrush. How unfortunate, he thought, as the car careered down the street and crunched into a lamp-post. The head of the villain at the wheel inside struck the glass. Phim was spread-eagled on the outside. He rolled off, somewhat shaken but unharmed, belly button tingling. The Corvette reversed and the engine coughed and stopped. Ange called out, Quickly, move away, Phim. They disappeared down a side-street.

Yaeli had a guitar and was singing a sabbath song. Lechah dodi, likrat kalah. Come my lover, welcome the bride. The sabbath day is the bride. The Lord is the bridegroom. It's an ancient Moorish melody. Sephardi, said Yaeli. Beautiful, said Irma. You can dance, said Yaeli. Put away grief. Be joyful. The queen is coming. God is one. Irma and Phim danced. Yaeli sang about Jerusalem being rebuilt. My people! Dress in garments of splendor. Guard and remember in a single utterance (Exod. 20.8; Deut. 5.12). Hashem echad ush'mo echad. God is one and his name is one.

Lecha Dodi ('Come my friend') hymn to welcome the Sabbath, comp. by Solomon Alkabetz (c. 1505-76).

Hold my hand, said Yaeli. Phim held her hand, and they walked through the cemetery. We're breaking the rules, Phim, since women and men are supposed to walk along different paths. This is where the great Kabbalists are sleeping. In this age, their wisdom is opening up to women more and more. Their strength is in my work. What do they say, asked Irma, looking at Phim holding Yaeli's hand, and feeling a twinge of jealousy. A secret, laughed Yaeli. I'll tell you as we visit the tombs in Tsfat. It's amazing what you learn.

Besieged from all directions, Phim was standing at the centre of three roads. There were unfriendly armed men marching towards him. Panic. Where could he go? Yaeli was speaking. Rabbi Moshe Inquizish in the Holy Land led the movement to re-accept Jews who'd been forced to become Christian. Many Jews rejected them, saying that they'd been weak. Looking at the armed men carrying iron shackles, Phim said, I feel so much grief. I cannot bear it. Sal said, What can we do? Yaeli said, Hold hands. It felt better holding hands. Looking at Sal and Yaeli the dark dream faded.

Rabbi Moshe Inquizish is a fictional name.

Yaeli had started talking about Kabbalah. The upper realm and lower realm are intimately connected in secret ways. These connections operate in every aspect of existence, extending to words, letters, laws, hidden concepts explaining the reality of God, mirrored in the earthly realm, in the soul, in the mind, affected by action for good and evil. The most important point is that God is present in totality, present in every mitsvot, present in every connection. This is the Jewish gift, this understanding. We find God by "reading" the lower realm; creation is a parable he gave us to find Him.

How, said Yaeli, did the infinite perfection of God create a temporal world of imperfection? Could God create imperfection? The Zohar, and commentary by Rabbi Yitzchak Luria (called the Ari) provided an answer. Creation is a contraction of the holy light of God, in a series of descending movements, filling vessels which contained his godly power. This was the mystically revealed truth behind Genesis. The problem was that God's light was too powerful for the lower world. The vessels shattered. Their repair is the work of righteous life. By obeying mitzvah, vessels will be able to hold the light.

You remember that God teaches by parable, said Yaeli (Ps 78.2). We do, said Phim and Sal. Ari elucidated a system of creation, with vessels shattering, with correction required, with choices made between good and evil, with soul ascending towards God. It's a map explaining the human soul. It's an interior life in which we have choice. In the beginning man was perfect. Rules got broken. Vessels shattered. Faith is the striving to be a perfect vessel, to hold God in our minds securely, and to be united with Him. Reparation. Restore Eden. This is achieved when we remain righteous.

Yaeli said, Kabbalists attempted to understand two aspects to God: a) God in essence, absolutely transcendent, unknowable, limitless divinity; and b) the manifested knowable reality of God, the creator and sustainer of humanity. Kabbalists talk of the first as Ein Sof "the infinite | endless." Human intelligence cannot truly grasp this. The second, the divine emanations, are accessible to perception, dynamically interacting through spiritual and physical time, revealing God. By reason, through language, we can understand something of Him from these emanations, and by understanding His revealed nature, we can glimpse something of His concealed mystery.

Yaeli said, When you know about the Kabbalah, the deep structures of faith are revealed. Take the idea of the Trinity, proclaimed at the Nicaea Council (325). The one God is described in three persons, a mystery, a paradox. Two persons are concepts from family life: Father, Son. Holy Spirit is different. In the Kabbalah, God is explained by the Sefirot, ten attributes (or emanations) working together. We meet them in the psalms. Wisdom, understanding, knowledge, kingship and others. Crown at the top, the Unknowable. Each requires special explanation. They are not separate gods. Understanding their interaction will explain God.

See dedication page for a list of sefirot.

The ancient text Shiur Komah presented an anthropomorphic image of God, said Yaeli. The ten sefirot were applied to it. Three sefirot for the head; two for the arms; sixth for the body or heart; two represent the legs; the ninth the phallus; the tenth a separate female power. This mystical image of God, with measurements for the limbs, portrayed the divine realm in dynamic terms. Sometimes the same sefirot were depicted as a tree. The anthropomorphic description of God remains a central issue for the Abrahamic faiths, whether verbal or pictorial. It certainly does, said Sal, and laughed.

Indebted to Joseph Dan, Kabbalah (OUP, 2007).

Of the ten divine powers shown by the Sefirot, said Yaeli, the lowest is considered to be female, the power of God that reaches to the created world. It is this power that the prophets hear, and it is this power that is taken away from us by the forces of evil. In the Talmudic literature Shekhinah refers to God, his presence in the Holy of Holies. It was considered to be "feminine" in later Kabbalistic development (Bahir, Zohar). Phim said, Human realities (masculine, feminine) are used to explain the divine.

Yaeli said, The Zohar teaches us that there are 72 holy names for God, revealed in three verses (Exod. 14:19-21). Each verse refers to a divine attribute (sefirot) of chesed (kindness, grace), gevura (might) and tiferet (beauty). The Zohar teaches that in the first verse the letters must be arranged in order, and the second in reverse order, and in the third in order. The letters can be arranged in a chart of 72 triplets. The Kabbalah is thus revealing from Torah that God has hidden names that we did not know, which are sanctioned. What's the point being made?

Inspired by "72 'Names' of G-d" by Moshe Yakov Wisnefsky (ref. to the Zohar II:51b).

Sal said, That's amazing because you know that Islam has the 99 names of God, which are all holy attributes. It's a prayer of great power to bring us to paradise. Beginning with God is the benevolent, the merciful (ar-Raḥīm), the judge, the friend, the loving-one, and continuing to 99. You sing the holy names. Instituted by Muhammad. One of my favorite prayers. I pray it always. Phim said, Teach me that prayer, Sal. It's good to think on ways we can know God. Sal said, Singing the prayer you focus on the unified power of God. It lifts you.

Sahih Bukhari Vol. 9, Book 93, Hadith 489.

Yaeli said, A vital Jewish teaching, intrinsic to Kabbalah, is the revelation of Hebrew letters. Alpha and omega the first and last, said Joseph (Isaiah 48.12; Rev 21.6). **Alef, said Yaeli. There are three strokes, an upper stroke, representing your heavenly soul, a lower stroke representing your animal soul. There is a line of balance between. Alef teaches us we must balance these two. Phim said, This sounds like St Paul's spirit and flesh. Paul's mistake, said Yaeli, was to try to cut off the flesh. To deny it totally. Sal said, We need to integrate them to be whole.**

Ideas adapted from "Alef Meditation," by Laibl Wolf of Melbourne Chabad.org.

The number forty is important, said Yaeli. Moses went up Mount Sinai for forty days. The Kabbalah teaches that reality can be divided into four worlds: Atzilut (Emanation), Beriah (Creation), Yetzirah (Formation), and Asiyah (Action.) These four worlds emanate from the four letters of the holy name of God. Four is a foundation. Four elements. A holy altar with four sides. Ten is God's gift, the ten commandments, the Holy Law, civilization. Ten sefirot. The Talmud says it takes forty years to understand the teaching. The number forty is completion. Through the gate of forty into happiness and peace.

From "Why Did Moses Go Up on Mt. Sinai for Forty Days?

The Significance of the Number Forty." By Yehuda Shurpin. Chabad.org.

Yaeli said, Someone asked Rebbe Shimon bar Yochai (in the Zohar) why God created humanity's evil inclination. The Rebbe replied, It was to merit either reward or punishment. (Deut. 30:15). Surely it would have been better without it, they said.   No, from chaos an ordered state was created. There is light and dark. You must choose the light. Partner with God. Consider the meaning of the first light created on the first day. Make your choice.   In doing good you clothe the Shekhinah in glorious robes. Where is the Shekhinah in relation to your righteousness?

Inspired by "Lighten Up, Partner!" From teachings of Rabbi Shimon bar Yochai; trans. & commentary by Shmuel-Simcha Treister from *Zohar*, p. 23a, based on Metok MiDevash. Chabad.org.

From the Jews, said Yaeli, the western world learnt how to read. There are four levels to reading the Torah. The plain sense Peshat; the hinting sense Remez; the moral sense Derush; the secret sense Sod. This four-level method was called Pardes, an acronym. Pardes means orchard, similar to the word Paradise. How precious a parchment was in ancient days; how important to have a teacher who could explain. To be given the delight of understanding! Wisdom is Paradise. The Christians and Muslims would follow this way. From this develops the world of allegorical poetry, the novel and allegorical art.

Water flowing on the rocks made a gentle sound to follow. Irma walking in front. Early spring, birds singing. There were wool mills built by Jewish settlers who had arrived from Spain (c 1500), now ruins. They stopped by the Shevchi pools, and ate sandwiches. Look at the flowers, said Yaeli. Cyclamen, anemone, hyacinth and asphodel. These are all native. In the sunlight they looked remarkable. Bright spirits lifting up their hands, thought Phim. How good that no one has picked them, said Sal. This is a Palestine oak, said Ange, some brown acorns still remaining from last year.

They had left Safed, and were driving past Chorazim. Where next? said Sal. Let's stretch our legs a moment, said Phim. It was an archaeological site. Blocks of black basalt covered with fine dust. What happened here, asked Irma. A wicked place, said Joseph. Jesus taught them but they threw him out. Phim was peering at a carved stone. It appeared to be a beast with long teeth, hiding behind some leaves. Two young men appeared, wearing black skin-tight running gear. One slapped Ange abruptly. They seized Phim under the arms, hauling him away. Don't resist, they said.

Phim yelled with full force, Sal! Help! Startled they released their hold. Phim sprinted away. A dusty road, late afternoon, few people about, Phim out of condition, the two runners closing quickly. Sal now in pursuit. Ange shaking his head and starting to move. The skin-tight runners grabbed Phim and belted him. Phim fell to the ground. Sal arrived. Sal very angry. Almighty right hook. Down he goes. Turned to the other. Seized him. Same again. Two on the floor. Phim got up, dazed, lifted his foot to kick, thought again. Muttered peace. Joseph shouted, Let's leave right now.

Yaeli and Irma were reading the paper. An article about students passing the entrance exams to study medicine. This is terrible, said Yaeli. In an African capital city, the leading hospital had doctored the results to ensure that the balance between male and female medical students remained 66 / 33 in favour of men.   They don't want women to dominate the medical profession, said Irma.   Stupidity is the true opponent, said Yaeli.   Let the gifted ones rise, let them marry, let their children achieve. We need to solve so many problems!   We need the best, said Irma, man or woman.

Phim was searching for music through YouTube on his iPhone. Tabors. Drums. Electric mandolin. Electric guitars. A wolfish young man was singing something in Hebrew. They'd put subtitles. It was a rock anthem. This is great, he said. Rocking to and fro. What is it, Yaeli? Psalm 150. Turn it up, said Sal. It's a band called Miqedem. Are they famous? When the lead sang the phrase "hallelūhū bəṣilṣəlê ṯərū'ā" (praise him with the clashing cymbals) a wave went through the Cruiser. Play that again, Phim, said Ange, who was driving.

Ange said, We sing that in Coptic. Joseph and Ange started chanting. Esmoo erof khen oo esmee en salpinghos. (Praise Him with the sound of the trumpet). It sounds like Greek, said Phim. Coptic was influenced by Greek, said Jo. You write Coptic with adapted Greek letters. The Pharaonic language in Alexandria evolved in a marriage with Greek. It became the sacred language of the Church. We still use it. The chanting was slow and solemn. We need the cymbals, said Irma. Pure joy. No Copt can hear them and feel sad. Phim searched on his iPhone.

Sitting on the balcony of a Rosh Pina bistro, admiring the view. Is that Mount Hermon over there? Snow on the upper slopes. Phim had a plate of meatballs to himself. A small slab of goat's cheese from Safed. A bottle of Yarden Katzrin Red Galilee (Golan Heights). Pitta bread, warm and soft. Olive oil on the tomatoes. Heaven, he sighed. Sal had ordered marinated roast mutton kebabs. Tender, he pronounced. They finished with a tarte tatin aux poires, with fresh cream. Perfect, chorused Yaeli and Irma. Cappuccinos. The evening sun had given a golden glow to North Galilee.

Phim stood in front of the Banias cave and thought about Pan. He remembered books that he loved. Peter Pan launching forth from the window followed by Wendy and the boys. What was that haunting passage, the piper at the gates of dawn? There'd been an interest in Pan in the nineteenth century, generated by the reading of the Gospels in Greek. Someone had said, That word "pan" (meaning "all" – used in the Gospel Greek) has a deeper meaning. Pan become Christ the shepherd? It was a great yawning mouth of a cave. Pan! shouted Phim. A faint echo replied.

The guide told horror stories. They sacrificed goats to Pan in the cave-pool. If the goat sank, it was accepted. If it floated, it was rejected. The cave-spring ran red with blood. Pan was a local deity in far away Arcadia. He'd arrived with settlers. There were few stories extant. Half-man, half-goat, playing the pan-pipes. Phim remembered British Museum amphorae. Graphic depiction of satyrs. Lust, pure and simple. Fertility and vernal life-force. It struck Phim that it was not goat sacrifice but surely wine poured out as part of a great orgy. Men were the goats, and the women?

Walking along the trail leading to the waterfall. A good path that ran beside boulders in the wood. Under arching boughs, now breaking into leaf. The Banias stream at its greatest strength after the winter rains. It sang merrily. Into the sunshine again over green grass. It was sunny. Irma found a tortoise, warming himself. Along the gorge, and then the waterfall, a tall white column of thunder. The snow melting from Hermon, all this water would flow into the Jordan and Galilee. Phim said, Listen! The voice of the waters. The roaring rush and peaceful crash of the waters.

With thanks to Sergio and Rhoda YouTube.

There was a robin on the post. What was it doing so far south? The others walked on, and Phim lingered to look at the robin. It started singing, thin fluting and hollow piping, stronger and stronger. Looking at Phim from left and right. Unafraid. Shouting at him. What are you saying, old chap? The bird sang on. Splash of royal red. Bright beady eyes. Pii piri pii didi dii didi dii. Is that it, asked Phim. The Robin cocked his head sideways and sang again. Phim heard a message. Watch out. The bad ones. Stronger.

65   March 5   Cable Car

They were in the brand-new cable car going to the summit area of Hermon. There was still snow but not enough for skiing. The cable car rumbled skywards. Views southwest towards Carmel. There were three others in the car. One of them took out a spanner and a blow torch, and started to open up the side of the car. In a moment he had cut a large window. He smashed it with the spanner and it fell to the snowy slopes beneath. The two other men seized Phim and tried to push him through the window.

Yaeli reacted very quickly, grabbing Phim's feet and pulling. Tug of war. The man with the blowtorch fired it up, and started brandishing it. Yaeli had to let go. Phim was struggling violently. He applied the blowtorch to Phim's neck. Keep still.   Phim yelled.   It was a stand-off. Two burly men in front, one behind, arm around Phim's neck. Sal thinking furiously. Jo, Irma and Ange facing.   Yaeli screamed full force. Very loud and painful. Irma did the same. Both of them together.   Astonishingly, the perspex-wall behind the men shattered. Sal and Ange leapt forward.

The two burly men were being pummeled mercilessly. Phim in grave danger. He was mean-looking. A vulture. Yaeli tried to land a punch. Joseph dodged the spanner, and grabbed his arm. Irma took her shoe and belted him around the head. Joseph pulled him to the floor. Yaeli knocked him out with a taekwondo kick. Meanwhile the cable car rumbled on, half open to the elements. Phim's neck was burning, and he felt very angry. For lack of rope, Ange and Sal had stripped the men. Shall I burn them a little, thought Phim, picking up the blowtorch.

Ange and Sal had stripped them and tied wrists and feet with their shirts.   Let me just write a little word on his chest, thought Phim, switching on the blowtorch.   Irma was watching, and said, Turn it off Phim, for goodness' sake. Let me look at your neck.   He had burnt through Phim's jacket and shirt. It was a nasty burn.   It will heal, said Yaeli.   The cable car was arriving. Joseph said, When we arrive, move away very quickly.   In a moment, they were in the descending cable car.   Ange said, Be more vigilant.

An ancient city in the far north, close to the Jordan source, claimed once to be David's, flourishing before the Assyrians. Near one of the gates a stele was found, with an inscription MLK YSRL. The words malak and melek are similar, said Yaeli. Canaanite city on the Damascus road, taken by Israel. A strategic fortress guarding the north: Phoenicia-Canaan west, Aram and Assyria east. Seat of judgement. Desecration by Jeroboam when the kingdom split. Banish the Levites. A wealth-creating sanctuary for me. There's the high altar, where we sacrifice bulls to Baal. I won't go near! said Yaeli.

1 Kings 12.25-31. Jeroboam.

Lush and green, not what you imagine to be Israel, said Phim.   Irma pointed at the fig trees. They'd be good.   Yaeli said, I'll tell you a secret. A ripe fig. Open it up. A red jewel. The outer is white and milky. Puzzle. What did he promise?   Ange said, It's true. The Dan stream is a torrent of cold pure water. There   were   some   Israeli   army observation posts and bunkers.   This is the gateway to Galilee. As long as men have been men, they have fought for possession. It's worth having. Two day's march, the sea of Galilee.

The Dan river rapids feeding the Jordan. Surprisingly loud and turbulent. Can anything be more beautiful than sunshine on white water, said Sal. The noise was tremendous. Voices were shouting in praise. Let me listen a moment, said Phim. They stood and listened. Let the sound fill my head, he thought. I can hear something, said Yaeli. Barakh shemo. Beshimkha. Over and over. The fire salamander they had seen earlier that day came to Phim's memory, holding up his fore and hind feet, grinning at Phim. Curious creature, four and five-toed. Brilliant yellow and black.

Phim was watching a videoclip. An Oxford scholar explained the evolution of the eye. How could such a complex organ evolve? Geological time, he said, a slow shuffle of cells finding answers. A light-sensitive band, a cup of cells finding light direction, a pin-hole camera. See-through cells formed a lens, greater light, sharp focus, the eye of a hawk or a dove. The human eye reading, writing, performing micro-surgery. Not convinced? In the animal kingdom there are survivals which show every step of the way. Flatworms with a cup, the nautilus with a pin-hole.   You're speaking Genesis, thought Phim.

With thanks to Prof. Richard Dawkins.

73   March 13   Our Fault

Yaeli said, Consider what Richard Dawkins wrote. "Natural selection, the blind, unconscious, automatic process which Darwin discovered, and which we now know is the explanation for the existence and apparently purposeful form of all life, has no purpose in mind. It has no mind and no mind's eye. It does not plan for the future. It has no vision, no foresight, no sight at all. If it can be said to play the role of watchmaker in nature, it is the blind watchmaker." Phim said, This beautiful truth is a bitter word. It describes our fault in the gift received.

With thanks to Prof. Richard Dawkins.

Sal said, The acceptance of the theory of evolution requires us to reconceptualize our faith. With one leap, everything we've been told is literally invalid. God does not intervene in history in the way they say. That knowledge was a stage.   Phim said, Yes, an allegory of truth. Still true, but modern science is the beginning of an advanced knowledge which allows us to begin to understand as God will understand. Gabriel says, Come with me outside your home. Look at it. A beautiful blue globe. Step by step I allow you to understand the miracle I give you.

Sal said, There's another way to consider evolution. Human society evolved to a new stage of knowledge. At the same time, the human brain changed. Now, we have education for all people. But in the ages of faith, it was only for priests. God is (and was) a teacher. Today, he gives to all. Faith evolved. Within faith there was development and revelation. Mary herself evolved. New orders were born. Now, the world is different. On this educational plateau can we be peaceful? Can we protect the gift? Can we save our world from ourselves, said Phim.

Yaeli, said Phim, I've seen something frightening in all this. I saw it before and put it aside. In the last 200 years we've gained an understanding that never existed before. We begin to know how and why and when. We see a vast intelligence emerging in humanity which assumes all the powers that we ascribed to God. We can heal leprosy. We can destroy cities. We can even control the weather. We possess the earth so fully. Yet we still do not understand the most important thing. Irma'am said, You're right, Phim, and it's our task.

With thanks to Prof. Richard Dawkins.

Mama Mia, said Phim, pulling off his black sandals, and scratching his toes. Ooh! Aah! he cried, extreme itchiness. Will you STOP that Phim, said Irma, trying to move away, but unable to do so in the confines of the Cruiser. Thank God, said Yaeli, that you're not wearing shoes. Phim had started peeling his socks off. It was a ghastly sight. Five white toes which had lived in darkness wriggled in the light. They needed a scrubbing brush. Sal said in a strained voice. Phim, stop scratching so much.

Irma said, Look at the flowers! They
were on the Lookout Trail in the
Yehudiya Reserve. A carpet of spring
flowers.   Yaeli and Irma were
competing to identify them. Is that
mustard? Yes, said Yaeli. Bright
yellow. A bee was gathering nectar.
That's star-shaped campanula. Look,
a Syrian cornflower. Inflorescence like
a blue firework. Corn poppy, said
Phim. A red shout to God. They
stopped, unable to identify a mat of lilac
flowerets. Bugloss, said Sal, surprising
them. It was clad in fine white hair.
Bugloss is Greek, said Phim, checking
his iPhone.

There were hyrax in the rocks, looking
nervous. They disappeared as Phim
approached. There was a picnicking
family sitting by the Meshushim pool.
Mother with her baby on the rock. The
stream flowed by her.   Join us, she said.
They all sat down to picnic. Tall
waterfall behind and the great pool
beneath. A man (who looked a bit like
Phim) smiled and said, Let's jump in the
pool. Phim stripped and they leapt in
together.   Pure water, he laughed.   It's
freezing, gasped Phim.   They shared
towels.   How do you feel?   Great.   He
had a thermos of hot tea.

It is not permitted to jump in the Meshushim pool.

Sal said, God designed this land. The holy basin of Galilee; the holy mountain of Tabor. A pool of miracle water hidden by hills; a natural tower that gives vision in all directions. Learn to love me my children! On a high place Adam, forgetful of Eden, found God again. How many hundred thousand years ago, our thought expanding and words exclaiming? The hill is clad in trees, precious resource for a carpenter from the village. How important it is to protect it. Yes, said Phim, we must plant trees. Here of all places a beautiful green raiment.

81   March 21   Eye

It was an airy church. The light from the windows strong. A cool breeze circulating.   Phim looked at a mosaic in a chapel apse.   It looks like Lord of the Rings, he joked to Irma.   An eye was set within a triangle, set within rings of a large flaming sun.   It's like Kabbalah, said Irma.   Three-sided unity, mused Phim. Is this also a puzzle? Is there a secret in this I have not found. Is there a scientific law hidden here?   He looked at the eye; the eye looked back.   Time, it said. Use it.

Church of the Transfiguration (Franciscan) Architect Antonio Barluzzi (1924).

They stood in the Greek Church of the Holy Transfiguration. It was brimful of icons. Every inch of space told a story. Christ frowning in judgement gazed from the skylight. His mother the Theotokos with arms upraised in blessing was enthroned above the altar. Her son stood blessing before her.   It'd take a week just to read and understand the walls, said Phim. Look, the healing of the man with a withered hand. Shush, said Irma.   A priest sang, a mellow baritone.   O Christ you are the true effulgence of the Father appearing with Moses and Elijah.

As they drove away from Mount Tabor, Phim noticed a sign saying Stone Jars for Sale. They parked the car. A man was selling stone cups to tourists, explaining that it was an ancient limestone quarry for stone used to make water vessels. Remember the story of Jesus and the wine, he said. Phim was interested. He explained. Stone vessels are exempt from the purity laws. They are not mentioned in Leviticus. They had stone cups, machine-tooled with doves and olives. 100 shekels. I'll take a couple, he said. Yaeli whispered, Don't be a fool, Phim.

Yardenit the baptismal site south of Lake Galilee. Yaeli said, The Greek word baptism is just a translation of the Hebrew concept of washing away sin (H7364). Joseph said, It's NOT just a translation. Phim said, There's continuity between the use of the Mikveh and Christian Baptism. We need to strengthen that continuity with love of God. There was a woman in the water wearing a white robe, singing out The Holy Trinity, and helping a young boy to immerse. He emerged blinking and smiling. She had a dove-like maternal expression. He must be about ten? asked Irma.

Exod 30.19-21; Leviticus 1.9; Psalms 26.6.

Phim was astonished at Beit She'an.   A
piece of puzzle.   There were records
that the Pharaoh Thutmose III had
conquered Palestine (c. 1450 BCE).
Archaeology confirmed this. Beit She'an
was the administrative capital for three
centuries of Egyptian rule. Like Rome
and Greece, Egypt had been a colonial
power. There was Phoenician presence.
Then Philistines. It enters Biblical
history as the place where Saul's dead
body was hung up.   The tell (mound)
was   formed   by   many   different
civilizations, as they had seen in Jericho.
The Romans chose to found a new city,
probably considering the original site to
be cursed.

This was the leading city of the Decapolis, their only city west of the Jordan. They strolled between tall columns down the reconstructed high street. The huge tell behind them. It was also man-made, layers of history. Like Jericho, an ideal location. Good climate, fertile soil, abundant water. Galilee a few miles north. The Jezreel valley led to the sea. The problem was that every invading army passed through. The Romans made it magnificent. Aqueducts. A huge theatre. Baths. Later, for a short time, Byzantine Christianity flourished. The town was destroyed by a massive earthquake (749 CE).

They were surrounded. They slowed right down. The flock was blocking the road. Then behind them a hundred more filled in. Where was the shepherd? Phim was driving. Delighted at the sheep, he wound down the windows. Powerful stench invaded the car. One of them, bold and curious, poked her head through the window, and said Blaah! Phim was startled.   Irma laughed. You've made a conquest, Phim.   It was a goat.   She continued.   Baa-baa bléeh-bléeh and nibbled at the driving-wheel.   Phim said, Shoo! Shoo! go back and join the herd.   The shepherd appeared, and slowly the flock moved aside.

As they drove away, Phim called out to the shepherd. Nice sheep! Thank you. What kind are they? Jacob Sheep, a resurrected breed. They're clever and hardy. Look at the horns. Some of them had four black horns, two on the top and two curling round on either side. There was one with two very pronounced horns. The fleece was parti-colored, brown and white. They looked like a cross between sheepdog and sheep. They used the best horns for the shofar, the ancient trumpet. With horns like that you could get caught in a thicket. You could, he said.

Genesis 22:13

They stopped at a petrol station to fill up. Phim got out of the car and stretched. He was still thinking about the sheep they'd met. Wouldn't it be nice to be a shepherd, looking after them day by day. He had to admit he didn't like the smell. There were no wolves these days. It must be hard to do the shearing without hurting them. He thought about the lambs, how lovely they were, what tender voices … As he was daydreaming, a white van drew up, grabbed him, and skidded off. Kidnapped again.

They looked like the same guys as before, in a bad mood. They cuffed him aggressively on the head and said, You misbelabeled piece of filth, we're going to send you on a journey. Phim was speechless. They had a brown samsonite suitcase which they opened in the back of the van. Get in. No. They cuffed him. Get in. No. They hit him hard. Dazed, he got into the large open suitcase. Curl up. He curled up. They closed it on him, and turned the latches. It appeared to be airtight. How many minutes could he survive?

Only a few minutes of air. He could scarcely move. The van was moving quickly. Phim felt for his swiss army knife. In the upper corner away from the handle, with great difficulty he drilled a little hole. Success! He would live a bit longer. The van stopped. They lifted out the suitcase.   Quite light, isn't he.   Are you dead yet?   Phim said nothing, hoping they wouldn't notice the hole. You're going south, corpse. Guess where. They laughed harshly and threw it in the Jordan. It sank briefly, and then floated. Phim's little hole was uppermost, a ray of light.

Phim was struggling to get enough air, worried about water getting in. He enlarged the hole. The river held the suitcase and slowly it made its way south. Providence had granted that it floated with his little breathing hole above. It was still dry inside. Phim remembered his iPhone. With difficulty he got it out and phoned Yaeli, the only one to have a mobile.   Phim! Where are you!   I'm in the Jordan, in a brown suitcase, going south. I can't get out. I'm all right. Drive south quickly and try to spot the suitcase. It's dark brown.

There was disbelief at first in the team. Phim explained. There was no time to lose. If the suitcase filled with water he would drown. Irma pray for me. Sal said, Phim, be patient. God holds you safe. We love you, Phim. What's the speed of the flow? About 5-6 km per hour? Yaeli now revealed her strength. She phoned the water authority, and checked on the Jordan water flow. Looked at the map, and calculated where Phim would be. He should pass by Tirat Zvi in thirty minutes. Route 90. We can be there in twenty.

They were there very quickly. Date palms. A white dusty track. Irma got out Phim's binoculars and scanned the river. Nothing. Yaeli rang Phim.   Are you OK Phim?   Yes.   Is it moving?   I think so. We're waiting to spot the suitcase.   Can you breathe?   Just about.   Hold on, Phim.   The river held him gently, the breathing hole upwards.   Phim started to sing.   Rule Britannia!   He thought better. A Negro Spiritual.   Roll Jordan Roll.   Sal peering up the river said, I can hear someone's terrible singing.   In the middle of the river, one corner aloft, Phim's brown suitcase sailed into view.

Phim, cried Irma, tears in her voice, and they all shouted together, Phim! He heard them. Never in his life had he heard anything so sweet. Irma, he cried, thank God! Ange and Sal waded into the river and grabbed the suitcase. Is that you Ange? They lifted the suitcase onto the track, and opened it. The villains had omitted to lock it. Phim took a lungful of air. It had taken about ninety minutes all told. He managed to stand up. I am lucky to be alive, he said. He wept in the relief and gratitude he felt.

As they drove away on route 90, Irma said, There's a scenic drive over Gilboa. They turned left onto route 667, driving north. Blue skies, beautiful spring weather. The ridge up ahead. Farmland either side, green and fertile. There were few cars. Ange at the wheel. The Cruiser stretched into a smooth steady run, the engine humming. Phim was glued to the window gazing at the peaceful landscape. Wasn't this where Saul lost to the Philistines? On Gilboa, up ahead, said Yaeli. David sang a tender lament for the death of Jonathan.

1 Sam. 31; 2 Sam 1.

Phim looked behind. There were four motorbikes, engines roaring. They were wearing black, with black goggles, and Endor! written in white on their helmets. Two of them had small automatic weapons. Ange, the bandits are back again. Ange said, I noticed. They appear to be armed. He accelerated, and the motorbikes pursued. There were cars coming the other way. They were waiting their chance. The road was clear. Two bikes moved ahead. Two came up closer behind, resting the machine guns on the handlebars. Ange muttered a prayer and hit the brakes.

One of the bikes went straight into the back of the cruiser, hitting the road, the man flying, automatic by the side of the road. The other bike shot forward. Ange stopped the car, dashed out, grabbed the automatic, got back in, and accelerated again.   Here Sal, can you use this?   As they drove through, rapid thuds struck the door. Splattering on the rear windscreen.   Paintballs?   Rapid-fire paintballs?   Ange skidded to a halt. Sal started firing at the other two motorbikes. They turned and fled. Ange reversed back to the remaining bike.

The third motorcycle fled. One lay on the road groaning, and they helped him to the side. He wasn't going to cause trouble. Then they looked at where the paintballs had hit the car and saw why they'd been unwilling to exchange fire. The paint had completely dissolved. Phim sniffed at it. Sulphuric. Paint balls filled with sulphuric acid? That'd be unpleasant. Sal, can you disable that weapon. Let's get rid of these acid balls first. There was a rusty old oil drum by the road. Phim, fire at will. So he discharged the paintballs into the drum.

The acid fizzled and then leaked away. Sal took the automatic and smashed it against the tarmac. They left it with the groaning man. Using the man's mobile they phoned a hospital and said there'd been an accident. Let's carry on, said Jo, they won't bother us now. Soon they were on the ridge. They stopped the car. On the left, a line of huge wind-turbines marched by. They rotated very slowly. To their right, looking NE, Beit She'an was below them, the Jordan, and the hills around Lake Galilee. A natural watchtower, said Ange.

They were driving through stands of forest clothing the slopes. Yaeli said, This ridge represents a triumph. In the 1960s, through the National Fund, many thousand trees were planted, and it was transformed. Yes, said Phim, a gift for the future generations, both Arab and Jew. So it is possible to change the world, said Sal. They had now arrived at a small park. A signpost said, Gilboa Iris. Irma, said Yaeli, have you ever seen anything as beautiful as this? A deep purple, almost black iris, lighter purple petals above with fine veins. A flower for a king.

There's a menorah. There's the ark. There's a zodiac depiction of the year. At the centre, the sun god Helios. There's Abraham obedient to God, about to sacrifice his son. How could you have such a blend in a synagogue? Joseph said, Romans became Jewish-Christian. Generations have gone by. The real Jews have left. They read the Bible in Greek. They love the teaching. They also love the old things of Rome. A little blending can't do much harm. It's Samaria, and it's my house anyway. It's good for conversation. One priest objects. Another agrees. Compromises. More people come.

They were watching a modern oratorio performed in Arabic. It was a religious allegory called "Creation." A rich bass-baritone sang a modern adaptation of the Bible verses of Genesis 1. Then a tenor and a contralto took over. There were the voices of Adam (tenor) and Eve (contralto) and the serpent (falsetto), and the first voice was God (bass). It ended with the expulsion from Eden. Adam faced the audience and cried the name of God in five languages.   Phim said, Wow! That was amazing. I want to hear it again.   Sal said, Truth has been told.

Phim was learning about Samaria-Sebaste on his iPhone. "The Israelites did not turn away from the sins of the house of Jeroboam, which he had caused Israel to commit; they continued in them. Also, the Asherah pole remained standing in Samaria" (2 Kgs 13.6). **Yaeli said, Jehoahaz** (c. 815-798 BCE)**, son of Jehu, did as Jeroboam** (c. 931-910 BCE) **had done in Dan. But history was written by Jerusalem. There was conflict with Aram and blending of culture. Joseph said, There's a connection here with Christ which runs very deep. Phim said, What is this Asherah pole?**

Phim said, I checked all the Biblical Samaria references. Bitterness. The Judah priests condemn them utterly. Then the Gospel. Jesus finds the Samaritan to be truly good. Irma said, It goes very deep. They thought they were foreigners. Jesus sees the heart of the people and knows their goodness. Is Samaria Hebrew, asked Sal. Yaeli said, It's Shomron. Ange said, Samareia in Greek. Samaria in Latin. It's connected to Mary in a secret sense. Joseph said, It might not be connected, but it is true there is sacred information in Mary's name, with many different meanings.

They were driving through Tulkarm
admiring the flowering date-palms.
There was a sign to a rose garden and
café. They stopped, and drank
peppermint tea. Early roses. Are
those Damask, asked Phim. He
walked over and sniffed. Wonderful
perfume. Sal said, A poetic symbol in
Islam. Isn't it too hot for roses? It
depends, said Sal. Phim noticed a
woman shake her bag onto the terrace,
and walk away. The bag said Crussadda.
A silvery object like a metallic centipede,
slid across the floor. Fascinated, Phim
went over. The woman stood apart
dialing up her mobile phone.

It was about a metre long, cunningly made with chrome scales, with minute internal engineering that allowed it to slither like a snake. It's a snake robot, cried Phim, astonished. Irma said, Get away from it you fool! It had no mouth or eyes. It paused a moment, and waved about, and then slithered rapidly towards Phim, quickly looping itself around his ankle. Irma was looking distressed. The head of the snake-robot then opened, revealing a syringe-needle. Phim saw what was going to happen but it was very tight on his ankle and could not be shaken off.

A drop squeezed out and fell on the decking. It went black. It waved about again, seeking where to strike. Phim grabbed it, and received a nasty electric shock. Irma seeing that Phim's death was imminent, smashed her handbag onto the syringe, disabling it. A jet of poison spurted up, a few drops striking Irma's hand. Ange was watching. He grabbed a watering can, and doused her. Using his handkerchief, Phim wrenched the serpent off and hurled it away. Yaeli pursued and severed it with a brick. Jo shouted, You half-wit Phim! Will you never learn?

A large square court around an octagonal sanctuary (Byzantine). The Samaritan guide asked for reverence. Phim was mistakenly thinking that this must be the ancient Samaritan Temple, the Holy of Holies in the centre. They walked around it, saying nothing, slowly pacing. He let his mind grow still and started hearing ancient voices. What were they saying? It was joyful. What language were they singing in? It seemed so familiar. Thanks be to God, creator of heaven and earth. It was deep within the mind. Round they walked, Sal before and Yaeli after.

They said that the ruins were all Byzantine Churches built on top of the original Samaritan sanctuary. What does this remind us of? asked Yaeli. Sal said, Dome of the Rock. A forest of pillars. Arches in festival stripes. Where were they? It was the true place and remained true. Joshua assembled Israel in Shechem. Covenant at the sanctuary (Joshua 24). They looked north. This is the blessed mountain; Ebal is the cursed. This appears green; that one appears barren. They go together, Phim. Are they protecting one another? Shechem which is now called Nablus lay between them.

Phim was reading about Samaritans. Descended from Jewish tribes. Survived the Assyrian capture of the ten tribes of Israel. Remained in Israel during the Babylonian captivity of Judah. Holding the Pentateuch as their scripture (the first five Mosaic books). Asserting Mt Gerizim to be the holy mountain of faith (not Sion-Moriah in Jerusalem). Despised and ill-treated by Judah Jerusalem Jews. Stubbornly surviving to the present day. Sounds familiar? Yaeli laughed, They're more Jewish than the Jews. What was the problem? Authority. Jerusalem could not permit an alternative centre. They say that Mt Gerizim is the centre of the world.

Is this true, Yaeli? The Maccabees destroyed the Samaritan Temple on Mt Gerizim? Yes, she said. They are Jewish heroes but there was a dark side. They enforced loyalty with harsh penalties. Sal said, Who are the Maccabees? Yaeli explained. Ange said, They were utterly opposed to Hellenism. But how good was that? There was a lot to be learned from Greeks. Joseph said, Antiochus IV (Reigned 175-164 BCE) put idols in the Temple (167 BCE). Greeks were destroying the faith. Mattathias and his sons became freedom fighters. The first act of defiance was highly symbolic (1 Macc. 2.23-26).

They had been allowed to stand at the back of the synagogue as they prayed. The men were wearing bright red fezzes. Some had white turbans. Most were dressed in white robes, one in vibrant blue. Two or three lifted silver poles between which the Samaritan Torah was held. They sang out the prayers extremely loudly, raising the scrolls as they did so. The synagogue shook with their voices. The walls sent back the sound like an earthquake. Praise and thanks be to God forever. Phim felt the chant moving his bones. His body was filled with their song.

Joseph said, Dothan near Shechem is where the brothers seized Joseph my namesake, threw him into a pit, took his coat of many colors, dipped it in blood, telling Jacob he'd been killed by wild beasts. They sold him to Ishmaelites. He was carried off to Egypt, walking by his mother's tomb near Bethlehem. Later, it is said that Moses and Joshua carried his bones from Egypt, and buried them here, at the foot of Mt Gerizim. Let us go there and pray together. They stood in the holy tomb. Saleem, Joseph and Yaeli touched the tomb, saying, Father Joseph.

With thanks to a presentation by Perry Stone. Gen 37.12-36; Joshua 24.32.

I'm hungry, said Yaeli, let's try some of the famous Nablus kunafeh. What is it, asked Phim. Designed for you, said Irma, laughing. Spaghetti-string pastry with syrup, layered with cheese, served like a pancake. A bit like sweet focaccia. A Turkish-looking chef with a white apron round a great belly said, Welcome! He brought a tray and served a pizza-slice for each. Coffee? Phim said, I fancy a long one. French? Good. The rest? Local is good. A harmony of honey-syrup, pastry and cheese. I could eat another one, said Phim, picking kunafeh out of his beard.

A small man with a white turban round a peaked green cap with a symbol on it stood with a group in the centre of the church. Phim looked at him, and looked again.   He was making animated gestures to emphasize a point.   It was a Sufi Peace Mission, using YouTube media to teach peace to the world by visiting holy sites. A man narrated the Gospel of John in Arabic as they listened on camera. The camera looked briefly at Phim. Phim was looking at the Sufi. He was dressed in green. Phim spoke to him saying Shukran.

A grey-bearded monk removed a stone cover placed over the shaft which went down, he said, forty metres. He lowered a metal bucket through the narrow opening. In ancient days, said the monk, it was deeper. It runs dry in the summer. The winch complained, an irritating screech. Why don't they put olive oil on it? thought Phim. The water looked good. They poured it out. Let's drink this, said the monk, saying thank you to God. Phim offered a cup to the Sufi, and he reciprocated. All drank. It was cold and refreshing.

In the shop they chatted to the monk. He had drawn many of the icons and dedicated his life to the beauty of the church. It had been restored a few years earlier. He showed them the stained-glass windows. The church is much brighter than most Orthodox churches because of the large windows. The elegant candelabra was also unusual with suspended stained-glass icons. He showed them icons of Saint Photina which he had made. Isn't she beautiful? She is overjoyed in her spirit. Her meeting with Christ makes her eloquent. She brings many to God.

Saint Photina is called Svetlana in Russian, said Ange. Joseph said, The Orthodox specialize in commemorating the early saints; the Roman Catholic generally commemorate later saints. Some people say that many early saints are legendary. The point is that each saint stands for a generation of martyred faithful. Saint Photina symbolizes the early church. Her story is linked to Nero, the monster of the early years. It may not be exact history, but it tells the truth. Woe to the Church under Nero (and similar monsters such as Diocletian). Joy to the Church in the coming of Helen and Constantine.

Phim watched as they made the olive-oil soap. The old man scooped out the hot yellow mash from the pool. The worker carried it downstairs on his shoulders. They poured it onto the floor of a large hall with windows. A man smoothed the paste with a trowel. They allowed it to set. It turned white. Wearing socks, they measured the floor into blocks, stamping each one with a mallet, not missing once. They built column-towers with the soap-blocks. Each one was individually wrapped in colorful paper. How much, asked Phim. Irma, would you like one?

Phim was talking to the Imam.   We'd like to learn something about Islam, to enrich our understanding of God.   The Imam said, What are you?   Phim said, The three Abrahamic faiths, Muslim, Christian, Jew.   In front of you, he said, pointing at the shelf. He gave them each a Koran. Chapter 82. He began to sing in a high tenor. Arabic, then English. When the heaven is cleft asunder, when the stars have fallen and scattered, when the seas burst forth … you will know of your good or bad deeds.   Judgement comes. Turn to God, said the Imam.

Phim said, That was beautiful. So we must prepare to meet God on the final day by living good lives?   Indeed, that is correct, said the Imam. Islam sings this line of warning the most beautiful of all, at first to the Arabs to turn them to the one true God, to obey him. It is given pure and strong. The Holy Book brought the diverse Arabian tribes to order and raised a great civilization. It was God's power come to us, repeated from before with the Jew and Christian, a special gift in the beauty of Arabic.

Phim said, Thank you for teaching me these good things. God bless you, amen. Please kindly sing another chapter if you may. The Imam smiled. Chapter 91. The Sun. Surat Ash-shams. It was melodious. Each line rhyming. The Imam's voice tender and strong. Then he sang in English. By the sun and its brightness, by the moon as it follows, by the day filled with brightness, by the night as it conceals, by the Heaven and Him who made it ... the gift from God is given to us. Shall you be wicked after such a gift?

Phim said, It is truly an enrichment to hear you sing. Can you kindly explain something about these chapters? The Imam said, At the end of time, after the general resurrection, facing judgement, what matters most will be the good and bad we have done in our lives. The verse teaches this truth. The word nafs, which means soul, refers to all humankind. Who are the watchers? Guardian angels. Maybe that is what WE are supposed to be, the Imam laughed. Please read Chapter 77 (Those Sent Forth) when you have the chance. Peace be unto you, he said.

They were indulging in Nablus Baklava, called fistikli. Heaven, said Phim. I could get fat here, said Sal. There was an elderly Turkish couple at the next-door table. Where are you from? Konya. We're revisiting our Palestinian roots. Many generations of our family lived here, but we were forced to leave in the turmoil. We built the town, developed the business, and brought peace and prosperity to the region for four hundred years. Phim said, People forget that. Come and visit us. There's a lot to discover. Thank you, said Phim. There'll be a lot to learn in Turkey.

Phim and Sal had come to the famous Nablus bathhouse. Face down, Phim couldn't see the masseur but felt fingers of steel plucking at the very roots of his being. Ow! Ow! he yelled. Don't be such a weakling, said Ange, who was there also. He said something in Arabic. The masseur continued. He took hold of Phim's shoulder and rotated it clockwise. Are you tearing me to pieces, cried Phim. In reply the masseur slapped his back, and Phim could say no more. He lay like a boneless fish. All the stress had gone. The mind was free.

Ancient puzzles preserved in holy letters tied to the land, said Yaeli. Nothing much remained. A pile of weathered stones in the sun. Maybe this isn't Shiloh, thought Phim. Yaeli continued. The Hebrew of the verse (Gen. 49.10) when Jacob says farewell is ambiguous. The gift teaches us find the truth by indirections. Irma'am said, Yes, it is always a struggle, just to understand, and then to decide. Phim said, The danger is that we render it too simple. Too obvious. True, said Ange. Joseph said, Retaining ancient elements might be part of the gift.

Shiloh is where Hannah prayed to the Lord, standing by the post in bitterness, said Irma'am. She had been tormented for being childless. Eli had observed her, seeing her mouth moving. He thought she was drunk. Sober up, he cried. Then he said, Go in peace. May the Lord grant your prayer. She bore a son, his name Samuel. He was dedicated to the Lord. Then she sang her praise-song: "My heart exults in the Lord ... There is no Holy One like the Lord; there is no Rock like our God."

1 Sam 1-1 Sam 2.1-11.

On route 60, in a few minutes they would be driving past Beitel.   Yaeli said, The guide says it's not certain that this is the Biblical Bethel – near where Jacob wrestled with the angel and saw the vision of the stairway, often mistranslated as ladder (Heb. sullam) (Gen 28.12; 32.24-31). It became a principal sanctuary. Later, it was given to the other gods. There was a process of rivalry and changing possession. Jerusalem became the official cult centre. Bethel was destroyed by King Josiah (c. 640-609 BCE).   Phim said, It says here that Beitin is Bethel. There's a ruined tower.

Whew, said Phim, is this potent. Taybeh Winter Lager the finest in the Middle East.   Stop reading the label, you idiot, said Irma.   Do you want a sip, asked Phim.   Not if you've drunk any of it. Yaeli laughed.   Cinnamon nutmeg honey ginger cloves.   Is that what they put in, asked Sal. It sounds like a curry. There was a beer connoisseur who praised it.   Phim took a swig, and crunched a few crisps.   Ah, he said, his head swimming a little.   Irma, won't you ever drink beer?   I don't like it very much, she said.

There was a festival in the town for Saints Constantine and Helena. They'd put up a stage and tables in the piazza. A band started playing. A young man sang in Arabic. What's he singing, asked Phim. A song praising Taybeh and its people. History of the two saints. A bouzouki came on, with tom-toms and flutes. Some local people and tourists stood up and started dancing in front of the stage. Let's join in. Come on Sal. Yaeli, Irma, said Phim. A swig of Taybeh Golden and they joined the happy throng.

There was a group from Japan with a stall which said, "Takoyaki." Phim wandered over. The electric guitars were loud and it was difficult to speak. What's takoyaki?   The man said, Octopus balls.   Phim wasn't sure he'd heard correctly.   Did you say octopus balls?   Yes, small round omelettes with a piece of octopus tentacle inside. Phim was amused.   I'll try one.   With chopsticks he maneuvred the yellow ball into his mouth.   It was very hot. Quick swig of Taybeh.   Chewy octopus. I'll have another. What's this green powder?   Nori seaweed.   It's good, said Phim. Where're you from?   Osaka, he said.

The only fully Christian village in the Holy Land? asked Phim. It sounds dire, said the young woman, but it's the truth. The proportion of Christians in the Holy Land has been in decline for a hundred years. Well, you could have a festival every month and generate wealth, said Jo. Celebrate saints. We have many Muslim visitors. You could celebrate peace heroes as a special theme. Pamphlet with a blurb. Arafat. Gandhi. Selassie. Shenouda. A monthly festival. We have to keep it secular. Pop and folk. Dance and song. How about comedy routines, said Sal.

The young woman, called Maria, told them about Taybeh.   We're in the OT and NT. In the OT our name is Ofra, a town of Benjamin (Joshua 18.23). We're mentioned in Saint John, a town visited by Jesus (John 11:54).   The Empress Saint Helena founded our first church, called St George. She also built the Church of the Resurrection in Jerusalem (Holy Sepulchre).   Saladin, after he conquered us in 1187, called us Taybeen (meaning good and generous people) because we (the Christians) watered his horses. We took the name. Here we are, she smiled.

Maria said, Come with me. I'll give you a tour.   Look, a traditional Palestinian house.   Stone   walls.   Farming. Shepherding. This family was quite prosperous. A raised floor for the living-room, one room for everything. Look here's the hearth. Underneath there's a stable space for animals, the larger animals there, smaller here. Behind the wall is a room for storage. In these alcoves, baskets for flour and vegetables. Normally there'd be a hole in the roof for air circulation, to let the smoke escape. Could it have been a house like this when they lowered the man on the stretcher?

Mt. 9.1-8; Mk 2.1-12; Lk 5.17-26.

Adapted from information on YouTube presented by Dr. Maria Khoury.

Maria said, There's greediness and we do suffer. They're given a huge amount of money. We have to live on scraps. A benefactor gives us water. Too many people. Too few jobs. Who wants to live in such a place – if it were possible to be happy somewhere else? In Taybeh we do share with our neighbors, both Muslim and Christian. I also endure the test – my patience stressed to the limit – can I say, God bless you and thank you? If I do, I'm a Christian, but what a test it is!   Irma said, I wish we could help.

Maria said, there's an event tonight outside the village. Come along. They were projecting the story of Saint George onto a large stone wall, part of an old church.   It   was   an   interactive computer-linked game. Saint George on the left and the dragon on the right. The dragon sent fireballs at Saint George and he deflected them with his lance. Players put on an electronic helmet. You had to concentrate your thought, focusing your prayer intensely. If you were good enough, Saint George would win. If you were weak, he got roasted.   How ingenious, cried Phim, let me try.

Phim stood there with the helmet on. God for Saint George, he cried, loud and strong. From the wall, George looked at him and smiled. The dragon withered, looking on Phim with a malicious eye. Tyrannosauroid, thought Phim, distracted. Out of the wall came a fireball, burning through him. Gasping, he took some water, and prayed. A beam of light from George's lance struck the dragon. The wall shook. The dragon roared. Phim prayed. Saint George for Palestine! George charged, and struck deep, reaching under the dragon's wing. Finish him, cried Ange, but the vision faded.

They were in the landscape garden of the new Palestinian Museum. A living guide to Palestinian flora, said Phim, reading the pamphlet. Here's a terebinth (Pistacia palaestina), said Yaeli. This was holy in ancient days. Bright red flowers. The resin produces turpentine used as medicine. This is mastic, said Ange. Fragrant resin. Ancient Greek chewing gum. We use it in the holy chrism. Here's a carob. Look at the black fruit, said Irma. These were Saint John's locusts. Husks for the prodigal. You can even make carob-chocolate. It's called goat's horn in Turkey, said Sal.

They were looking at an exhibition called "Motherlands and Dreamscapes." There was a painting of a mother and infant son.   I like this modern icon, said Ange.   A mother held her son close to her, her head resting on his head, gazing tenderly downwards, with her eyes making a vertical line. She was wearing a Palestinian thawb, with embroidered chest panel. It was framed by green vines and grapes on a gold background.   Within this she was enveloped by a body-length black and white veil.   Phim said, It looks like a map. Is this the shape of the West Bank?

Painting by Nabil Anani, Motherhood, 1995, Oil on canvas.

The problem, thought Phim, is how to bring wealth to Palestine. Look at those Israelis. Artists' studios all over Galilee. There's the constant stream of tourists. Someone always buys a picture … How about painting tree icons. Focus on the trees of Palestine and paint a portrait in oils. Best quality. Paint the personality. Bring out the holy gift. Paint it so that a pilgrim will put it on their wall. A Holy Land Tree. Link to ecology. For each icon I donate 10 dollars. Sal said, Trees are certainly holy. The ancient olive. The beautiful palm.

They were looking at an exhibition about Palestinian dress. This was the clothing of the Fellaheen, the Muslim peasants, said the guide. Look at this embroidery. A vivid red gown with long sleeves. White flower patterns. A chest panel (qabbeh), with a flower border. Under the veil there was a fringe of coins. Look at that, said Irma. It was a fez made of coins, with a long white veil behind. The guide said, That's Turkish influence. A bride might wear that. Her dowry. The workmanship was vibrant and joyful.

With thanks to Maha Saca, Palestinian Heritage Centre Director.

They were in a room of modern dress designs. A woman from Scotland was wearing a thawb, woven with dyed wool, with traditional patterns. She explained, We've come from the Hebrides to share our expertise in weaving Harris Tweed and tartans, to develop fashion-house products. Irma examined the thawb. It had wool strands of many colors, slightly rough to feel but also supple and strong. Embroidered patterns suggested flowers. The wool's a blend, she said. Sheep, goat and camel woven together, specially softened. It was a beautiful dress. How much? My goodness, said Phim, that is not cheap.

A wall of old Palestinian photographs.
Old postcards. The rich and the poor
together, said Sal. Subsistence versus
wealth and culture. Look at these
Bethlehemite women. They wear the
inner hat and white veil around. Old
clothes, scruffy children. Armies come
and armies go. We lose our land. Moved
here and moved there. We find some
way to survive. Yaeli, what's the
Hebrew for poor ones? Anii. Is it the
same in Arabic? Al-masakin, said Sal.
This gives Italian and Portuguese
meschino (76:8-9). Yaeli said, That
might be also Hebrew (Eccl. 4:13; 9:15-16).
Tubaa el masakin belruhe, said Irma.

As they drove to Ramallah, Phim was daydreaming, thinking about the Nablus soap. Design a soap from the Holy Land. Olive oil from the hills. Aromatic oils and resins from arbors of native trees. Essential oil from the Aleppo Pine. Extracts from the fig to give a unique fragrance. Lavender, thyme, citrus, myrtle, rosemary. What about flowers? Damask Roses? Give them a sachet of herbs? Top-end product produced by the water, sun and earth of the Holy Land. If I was a pilgrim, I'd get one. What would I call it? Wash-Off-Thy-Sin?

They must've have practiced for hours, said Phim, watching the Palestinian scouts band marching down the street in perfect order. They looked splendid wearing white shirts with red berets and sashes. The pipes were wailing "Angels we have heard on high." That's a bit early, said Jo. There were four young women twirling sticks and striking drums. A great musical phalanx moving grandly down the street. In a surge of enthusiasm, Phim walked over and started marching with them. He raised his reedy tenor. Gloria, in excelsis Deo. In a moment he was in the midst.

Quiet place, thought Phim, as they walked in the suburbs. Daydreaming about bringing in prosperity. He noticed garbage tipped down a slope. The covered market was a joy. They need tourists. How about a casino with big bonanzas? All profits go to preserving heritage-sites. Ramallah Las Vegas. How to appease the wrathful Imams? Class it as a special charity. He placed the chips. The ball spun round. Call it Peace Casino, he thought, and chose 8. The ball span on 48 and then rested on 8. An avalanche of green chips poured through.

They were watching a basketball team, after meeting a coach called Hakeem. They were all girls, wearing black. One or two hijabs. Christian and Muslim together. He started yelling in Arabic. Ange laughed.   He called her a dim-witted sheep.   A goat with three legs could do better.   Now he's calling her a blindfolded monkey.   The young woman looked mortified and the ball went into the net.   That's better! shouted Hakeem. You're a superstar! The girls huddled together, put their hands in the middle, and gave a shout.

What exactly is a shawarma? asked Phim. The café owner explained. The Turkish word for this upright turning spit is rendered shawarma in Arabic. The meat is sliced off, and garnished with pickled turnips or gherkins, and dressed with tahini or hummus. Depends on the meat. You won't find pork. Served in taboon bread or pitta. They ordered one each with a variety of fillings. Phim had mutton. You should set up in London, he said. I have family there, the owner said. They send money home. Have this, he said, and gave Phim a free slice of beef.

Sitting in an Italian café in the morning, Phim felt a powerful urge to drink a glass of wine. Irma, can you ask them if they serve wine? Don't drink wine, Phim, said Sal, it's only 11 o'clock. Dry white would be perfect, he thought, remembering student days in Italy, the joy (the madness) of drinking white wine for breakfast. They do serve wine, said Irma. One glass please. The wine was yellow-green, and chilled. Here goes, said Phim, Salute! Oh, it bit his throat with a sour harshness. Oh, it rasped his nose with a sharp acidic stink.

They left the café and walked among the crowds. Nice atmosphere. People were friendly. Phim was thinking it would be good to make friends and stay for a couple of years. Maybe I could learn Arabic? It would be nice to get to know them. Maybe I could teach English? There was a woman in the crowd watching them. Blond shoulder-length hair. Shocking pink T shirt with the message War Wanted. She pushed past them and Phim tripped on the paving, twisting his ankle. He heard something tear. Excruciating. He crumpled and waited for it to subside.

A student in the café invited them to visit the nearby Blind School. She explained. It was the only school in the West Bank that taught children to read braille, and kept a library of braille books.   This   is   the   old   braille typewriter. You type in Arabic Braille. You read it left to right turning the dots into Arabic. Now we've got computers and software. You can print out Arabic braille pages directly. But we all need fluent English, to read and listen to. There's so much useful information. Would you like to teach English to us, Phim?

Hakeem said, These are ancient trees. I know who I am when I look at them. These olive terraces were built by the fathers. Look, they still give fruit – giving to the poor without asking. We were the poor. We still are. They were in a village with an ancient oil press, huge millstones grinding the olives. Hakeem showed how they would layer the paste onto round fibrous mats, piled one on top of another, and a great press applied. This is where the oil comes out. The harvest is in October, he said.

Last day in Ramallah, they were sitting in the Stars and Bucks café. At the table next door sat a woman with white-rimmed sunglasses, a beaming smile, a red hat. Where you from? They chatted. Come with me, she said. The following day they went with her to the wall near Qalandia. Barbed wire on the top. Put your hand on the wall, Phim, she said. He did, and heard them. Arabic & Hebrew; Latin & Greek. The poor pay, she said, but God loves them. Remember that. She walked quickly away.

Through the checkpoint they could see tall cranes waving their arms about. It was a grand development.   Phim asked one of the men in the line.   They're building a mega-mall.   High-tech, dozens of stores, space for traders from Israel or Palestine.   They got a huge grant from US and Saudi companies. It's to show the next stage of peaceful coexistence and prosperity.   It's the dream, thought Phim, to shop in safety and peace, without anxiety, to have enough to afford something nice. When we achieve it we do not appreciate it but it is the dream.

They'd come to Beit Shemesh, a city
that flourished in the years after
Solomon, west of Jerusalem.   Phim said,
Samson's name came from Shemesh,
meaning sun.   Yaeli said, Samson was
strong but also passionate. Like David,
he had mighty hormones. He was also
funny. He defeats the Philistines with
the jaw-bone of an ass. Is he saying that
he's the ass? Is it his prayer? Or is he
braying at them? In the Hebrew there's
also a pun.   Ange said, He pulls down
the pillars of the wicked god Dagon.
The good son sacrifices himself for the
family.

Judges 13-16.

As they walked between the vines, a lion suddenly appeared, stopped and stared at them. They froze in surprise. Ange said, Don't move, and stood in front, looking around for a stick. A tawny old lion. The long mane had grey. He looked thin. Phim stepped forward fearlessly and focused his thought. The lion lay down. Put me back in the zoo, it's terrible out here. He looked imploringly at Phim, and managed a feeble roar. He was hoping that the keepers had come to feed him. He'd been dreaming of a tender young ibex for more than a week.

The lion turned out to be tame. The zoo-keepers arrived with a van. What a relief he was not shot, said Phim. Yaeli said, Samson's lion was a puzzle. He was strong enough to kill it with his bare hands. Irma said, It's a favorite passage. Pure poetry. Jo said, There's more than one meaning. Phim said, The lion is bad, but perhaps the lion is also good. Is it Samson with long hair? Is it his weakness for women? Yaeli said, Bees would only hive in the rock. Samson's teasing us.

Irma said, These stalagmites look like trees.   More like mushrooms, said Phim.   Cylinders and tapering pillars seemed to change shape in the electric light.   He thought for a moment there were eyes peering from within the fissures. The long dangling stalactites looked like the thin legs of a young girl struggling to get free from the roof. Thousands of years of water.   This is the true holy temple, said Sal, made entirely by God.   Angels, said Yaeli, alive in the imagination.   Softly she called out Halleluhu.

Irma had discovered a Marian sanctuary west of Jerusalem, not far from Beit Shemesh. There was a festival. They decided to spend a couple of days. They went first to the sanctuary. There were banks of flickering candles. On the ceiling angels flew between looping ribbons of salutation crying Ave Maria in a hundred languages. An angel carried a torch for fervor. There was a crowd gathered in front of the stage. Religious sisters, priests, Franciscan brothers robed in black and brown, and a squadron of the Knights of the Holy Sepulcher with bright red Jerusalem crosses.

Deir Rafat, Feast of Our Lady, Queen of Palestine Oct 29.

A green statue of the Blessed Virgin wearing flowing robes. Phim admired it. It reminded him of an ancient caryatid he had seen in Sicily. The Church was not hiding the connection, and the green power within the Mother was an ancient hope. Beautiful Mother, through you we have received abundant harvest. Our love for you remains, and by you it is united with the Father. Beside the statue on the processional bier there was a large palm branch resting against a pillar. It was decorated with yellow and white flowers. A constellation above the Virgin.

Festival is in October – this sequence in the wrong season.

Mary held out her hand over the choir. Phim was wishing once again that he could understand. They sang Kyrie Eleison, followed by Arabic Ya Rabb Arham. Spirit of reconciliation? It was life. The priest was calling the Christian faith to flourish in the land of its birth. She is our mother. The earth is an angel in heaven with the Love that created her. Grant us peace and stability, O God. Let us restore this land to beauty. The pilgrims will stream through. There will be work to do, more than enough.

The procession wound round the precinct in the bright sunshine, the band striking up a joyful melody as they sang Ave. The green statue walked above them on the shoulders of the throng. They were all garbed in different robes according to their orders. All is poetry, thought Phim, here the Mother symbolizes the love and unity in the people, our purity after the Holy Eucharist. What makes a place sacred? If anything, it must be our prayers, the prayers of the ancestors who sang and prayed as they ascended the hill.

In Abu Ghosh there was a huge crowd gathered around a giant satellite dish pointed at the heavens. What are they doing, asked Phim. They wandered over. It was a hummus restaurant. They were trying to win the world record for making the biggest dish of hummus in the world. A man stood there with a badge which said, Guinness Book of Records. They started pouring in the hummus. Crazy things people do, said Phim. What's going to happen to the hummus, asked Sal. The owner said, We're going to sell some and freeze the rest.

Inspired by event at Abu Gosh Restaurant.

Gradually the dish filled up. The crowd milled around, buzzing with interest. The Guinness man was taking notes. They finished filling up the dish. How much does it weigh, asked the official. One thousand pounds, said the owner. They confirmed it. He had won. Family congratulated him. A couple of rat-like skinny characters emerged from the crowd and moved towards Phim. Before anyone could stop them, they'd lifted him up and thrown him in. It was slippery. He tried to stand up and fell on his face. He lay there, up to his ears in steaming hummus.

They sat sipping chilled grape juice. There was a man with a luxuriant salt and pepper moustache. Are you feeling happy, he asked. He was the mayor. This town, he said, is unusual. We have inter-ethnic harmony. There's none of that conflict. The problem we have is how to maintain prosperity for all the children. Jews from Jerusalem come to us, a Muslim town, to listen to a Christian oratorio. We stand for high culture, high education. We've said goodbye to the ignorance. If this were real, thought Phim, for the whole of Palestine, what would it mean?

Amazing voice, thought Phim.   They stood listening as Brother Oliver OSB filled the Notre Dame crypt with a perfect fluting alto, an ancient falsetto singing the holy name of God high and sweet, Dixit Dominus.   Look, someone has rubbed out the faces of the apostles. Oh dear, said Sal, ancient hooliganism. Christ blessing from on high with the Virgin in royal red had survived better. We hold concerts here in the crypt, he said, you'd be surprised at the quality. That's the key. We approach the height in the best endeavor of art. We can share that.

Brother Oliver explained. This is an
ancient place. It was a village 8,000 years
ago founded on a spring. It's identified
with Kiriath-jearim, where the Ark of
the Covenant rested during the time of
David (1 Chron 13.3-8). Luke calls it
Emmaus, where the disciples see Jesus
in the breaking of the bread (Lk 24.13-35).
The Hospitallers (Order of St John
Malta) founded the present church. A
unique feature is the mixed Latin and
Greek inscriptions on the frescoes. This
was possible owing to a window of
reconciliation (1160-1170). Can you sing
again, asked Phim, it was utterly
amazing.

Brother Oliver said, You're welcome to stay. We have a guesthouse. Please attend our office and pray with us at least once a day.   Wonderful, said Phim. Irma and Yaeli with the sisters; we're with the brothers.   To their surprise, they were sharing the guesthouse with two Buddhist monks, from Korea and Japan.   They said, We were told to seek alliance with Benedict in the Holy Land. A brother had a dream which showed the destruction of spiritual life, both East and West, throughout the whole world.   Phim was surprised.   Was this a reminder of the task?

Phim was standing with the Buddhist brothers in the crypt. Oliver was singing again. Recordatus misericordiae. They smelt fragrant to Phim. He felt curiously attracted to them. Their shaven heads gleamed in the candle-light. Their faces were suffused with peace and love. They were praying their own prayers as Oliver sang. What are they praying, thought Phim. Can I connect, he thought, suddenly a hall opened up, the floor was golden-yellow, the voices hummed like a cloud of bees, a wave of joy lifted within him, peace and strength in the body, we are goodness. Sangha he heard.

They sat in the garden. Oliver said, 60 years ago a brother started interfaith outreach but it lacked commitment. There was little love in it. Lack of trust has always been the problem. Phim said, What about the Baha'i people? Oliver said, We don't need new faiths. They require us to merge and disappear. A better way is to strengthen one another. It requires real goodness. True, said the Buddhist. We will learn your virtues and love you; will you learn our virtues and love us? Phim was startled. He simply didn't know anything about them.

What do you mean by love, asked Phim. The Japanese brother explained. We teach meditation, which is a holy instrument to open inner goodness and rise above corruption. Love is the paradox at the core. Phim, I'm not supposed to reveal our secret-puzzles. I will say: the teacher came from far away, impelled by love, to risk his life to teach the people who had no knowledge. He knew their suffering. Sit still. Win peace. I will give you laws and teach you letters. My children, I will pray for you always. Is not this love, he said, and smiled.

The monk continued. I'm from Mount Hie in Kyoto; he's from Jogyesa in Korea. There was a brother in Dharamshala who'd had the dream. The message was: Go to the Holy land. Meet Benedict in the Ark town. The shining one taught them there. Find a donkey who can help. We think we found him, he said and smiled. Me? said Phim, feeling amused and annoyed. Come to Japan with us. Help us to destroy this nightmare. They described the dream. It was a mirror-image of the dream that Joseph had endured. We need you Phim, said the monk.

Phim said, How can I, or rather we, come to Japan?   Then he told them about what they were doing.   A wave of doubt possessed him.   He calmed himself, and looked at them. Two brothers. Shaved heads. One quite thin with high cheekbones. The other with a slightly pink round face. Beautiful robes. They had suffered in their discipline, but he felt nothing from them but peaceful love.   The round one said, The wisdom you will win, in comprehending our knowledge, completes your task. Nobody else spoke.   Phim said, Then we must go to Japan. Let's talk more.

Phim said, We can't abandon our present journey. Let's keep in touch. There's a current of spirit which tells me you are right. We have to learn more, and place the knowledge side by side, and resolve this paradox of the gift of life and heritage, so different, so multiple, so many thousands of years, and yet the Eternal Love is always one. They exchanged details.   We'll pray for you, Phim.   We'll send you strength. Link to us in your need, any time day or night.   They left.   Phim thought, Strange how help appears.

As the Buddhist brothers walked away from the monastery, Phim saw a dark grey mist swirling around them from left and right, and voices shrieking with hate and horror. The brothers bowed their heads. In their hands they held their beads, and sang a holy prayer. The ghouls massed about them, whipping them with long white cords studded with nails. Aaah, sighed a brother. Phim started running towards them, yelling with all his might, Begone foul demons! I love them! He shouted and the mist shattered. The brothers bowed, and carried on. Sayonara Phim, they cried. Come to Japan!

As they drove away, Phim said, That was an important encounter. Those two brothers come from a different time-line. I felt their goodness. In the world there is evil. It rose before our eyes. Here from this ground. How much blood was spilt! Phim looked back at the crusader church. Good Oliver stood guard. As they waited at a crossroads, a large truck accelerated towards them, and smashed the Cruiser into an ancient olive. Ange hit the windscreen. The truck backed off and drove away. Ange concussed. No one hurt? The Cruiser was a write-off.

Back to the monastery. Oliver was helpful. You can stay if you want. Talked to the police. Cruiser was finished. Insurance? It would help. Phim? Still got some of the fund left. Yaeli said, I want to stay with you guys as you go onward. Let me help. I've got some savings in New York. Phim said, Thanks Yaeli, you've become so important. Oliver said, There's a dealer in Beit Shemesh, but a benefactor gave us this. He took them to the garage. It was an enormous forest-green Mercedes Benz G-Class Off-road. We're not using it. How much, said Phim.

Sal, who'd found the Cruiser cramped, looked pleased. It'd been modified to seat six. Powerful engine. It'll be expensive, he said.   Oliver said, We won't be using it. Why don't you give me a couple of thousand dollars, and it's yours. We'll use the money for the monastery.   Done, said Yaeli. I'll pay, Phim.   Thank you, said Irma.   Oliver arranged for the wrecked Cruiser to be picked up. They did the paperwork the following day. Yaeli was the owner. She drove them away. Phim was sad to see the Cruiser go. White chariot to Jerusalem, thank you.

It had been an illegal squash in the Cruiser for a long time, so it was a relief to have a seat to oneself. Sal in particular had from time to time found it difficult being pressed up so close together. It never bothered Phim. He was secretly regretting it a little. Cruiser sandwich with ham, cheese and sliced tomatoes. Would I be the cheese, he thought, and felt a scratching tickling sensation on his big toe. He looked down. A very large brown cockroach was waving its antennae over his toe. Phim had a horror of cockroaches.

Phim was unwilling to stamp on it. How to get rid of it? He knew the cockroach rule. Where there's one, there's a hundred.   Who was it that said that – When the world had fought itself to oblivion, when the forests were gone and the seas dead, the cockroaches would survive, picking a living from the waste. Phim was inclined to class them with the locust. Perhaps they're not? He bent down to peer at it and quivered with disgust.   Cockroach, he cried.   Yaeli shrieked, There's one here.   Irma groaned, Three, no four.   Sal said, Two dead.

Get me in a bath, cried Yaeli. Ange
said, Let's stop in Beit Shemesh, find a
drugstore and get something that works.
They parked the Merc and asked for the
best cockroach eradicator. The choice
was a cardboard house with a sticky
floor, or a pesticide spray-can. The spray
was instant death. The house trapped
them alive. Spray, said Ange and Sal
together. House, said Phim. If we
breathe the spray it will be poison. The
cockroach house was made in Japan by
Earth Corp. It was called Gokiburi
Hoi-Hoi. One under each seat solved
the problem.

They filled up with petrol. Yaeli wanted to give the car a clean. They bought sponges and car wax. Here you are, Phim.   The garage lent them a vacuum cleaner. Yaeli, with an angry expression, hoovered every corner, catching a couple. No quarter.   Ange and Sal lent their muscle and soon the car was looking good. It was square-shaped, and long in body with a total of six seats. German   Super-Landrover,   said   Sal. Special   features.   All-round   radar. Satellite   navigation.   Internet.   Bose speakers. CDs. Look here's Benedictine Gregorian.   Put   it   on,   said   Phim. Miserere mei, Deus.   Is that Oliver?

It says that the name Ein Karem means spring of the vineyard or generous spring, said Phim.   Saleem said, The one who is eternally giving. Al-Karīm is one of the 99 names of God.   How was this place discovered to be Elizabeth's home, asked Irma'am.   They must have been close to Jerusalem, said Ange. Inspiration from above, said Joseph. An ancient holy spring, said Yaeli, she was Aaron's daughter, wasn't she?   A runnel from within the rock poured through three openings into a stone trough, called Mary's Spring. The sound was musical. They stood and listened.

How many churches are there, asked Irma. About ten, said Phim. It's a bit confusing. The Franciscan Church of the Visitation celebrates the meeting between Mary and Elizabeth. This was Elizabeth's summer home. Franciscan St John Church and Monastery is built over the birthplace of John the Baptist, which was a cave. There's also a Greek Orthodox St John Church. The Russian Orthodox have the Gorny Women's Monastery, part of their Jerusalem mission. St Vincent de Paul Sisters have a care home for disabled. A pilgrim guesthouse is called Casa Nova. There are other sister convents.

Irma phoned through and booked rooms in the Notre Dame de Sion Convent on the hillside of Ein Karem. High walls all around. It was peaceful. Phim drew a great breath. Let's stay for a couple of days.   Sister Marika guided them. They stood in the tall chapel. A thin gold cross on a white apse. She sang the Pater Noster. Her voice echoed brightly. Old olives in the compound. Ancient terraced gardens outside. A cloister to walk along within.   Spend today quietly. Tomorrow morning you must study the Psalms with me. I will teach you the Hebrew word beshimkha.

Psalm 100.2 H8057 bəśimḥā with gladness.

They stopped to admire a statue titled Magnificat (1947-8). Mary in a closely fitting veil showing only her face, looked downward with a visionary gaze. She held infant Jesus up to her left shoulder. His head rested against hers. Her right hand held up his left hand in blessing. Her long robes flow downward in elegant straight lines.   Phim said, What's that long belt that hangs down beneath her arm. It's got a buckle on it, and rows of studs.   Irma peered at it. Yaeli said, It's a loop. Is that a scutcheon?   Joseph said, It's an allegory.

Sister Marika explained. It was Vatican Two the revolutionary Catholic Council of the 60s. The declaration Nostra Aetate (1965) defined a new attitude to Jews. It spoke directly to our congregation. The world was asked to promote love through deep biblical study. We were founded by a Jewish convert, whose brother had a mystical encounter with Mary. We were friendly to Jews and Muslims, but after the Council our charism gained new strength. The Church would seek rapprochement with the Jews. We would find our Christian roots in Judaism. In our teaching and study we fulfill this vision.

Cool light-blue Spanish tiles, said Phim. The church belongs to the Spanish throne, another Antonio Barluzzi design (1939), incorporating former churches. They stopped to admire the large oil-painting of the Baptism set above the grotto where John was born. Father with beard above, cherubs left and right. White dove below. Jesus head-bowed, ankle-deep in the Jordan, holding a robe around himself. John with staff pouring a dish of water on his head. No full immersion here. The people make gestures of wonder. Peace and joy reigns. A green oak flourishes to heaven. Was it Murillo? How gentle Jesus appears.

Franciscan Saint John Church.

A Franciscan brother stood there in black robe and white cord.   If you wish, I can allow you to visit the ancient crypt, normally off-limits.   Thank you, said Phim.   He unlocked a doorway grill. They descended into the rock, down ancient stairs. A burial chamber dug from the rock. A trough in which a body was placed.   The brother said, Perhaps 1500 years old. There's something else. In another part of the compound they descended to an ancient mikveh. Perhaps 2000 years ago, said the brother. Is this a message, thought Phim, there a grave, here a pool?

It says that the Franciscans had a long struggle with the local Muslims to establish the monastery and church in the seventeenth century. But how could they exist there if the Muslims didn't want them? Sal said, We glimpse the ancient politics. The local peasant population was mostly Arab (some Christian). The elite-class was Ottoman Turk or Turkish appointed. The Franciscans would have given them a rich gift. They say OK. You can build. Local Imam hostile. Grassroots anger. Peasants say No! Also, the peasants don't like the Turks. Arabs and Ottomans have bad opinions about each other.

The small Greek Orthodox Church was closed. It had been built in 1894 and showed a perfect Romanesque form. Classical triangular pediment on the front like a Greek temple, on which an arched bell tower had been placed. The doorway was a tall arch within an arch. Sky-blue door. The floorplan was a cross. Phim walked around it in procession with Joseph and Angelos who sang a Coptic prayer. It served the Greek Orthodox for Sunday worship. Phim imagined the icons shining within as they sang the holy liturgy.

Mosaic on the church facade as they entered the gates. Phim stood and admired it. Exsurgens. Mary rose up. (Lk 1.39) Three angels swam in the air above her as she made her way to visit Elizabeth. Mary in profile looking Greek. An angel on her left and two on her right. The donkey plodding along patiently, eyes on the road. Elizabeth waiting up there at the gate. A Victorian storybook illustration worked into a brilliant mosaic (1955).   Phim looked at the donkey and thought, He knows he's carrying Jesus. On we go, slow and steady, climb the hill, mustn't slip.

Franciscan Church of the Visitation (1955), formerly St John Church.

Look at that picture, said Irma, Mary smiles in joy as Elizabeth cries out that she is blessed among women. How happy they seem. Elizabeth herself is six months pregnant. It pulls deep, said Yaeli. Becoming a mother is a holy blessing. You could say that every little child is Jesus, said Irma. In the lower church there was a fresco. The Holy Spirit as a dove poured down upon Elizabeth bending towards Mary. They held each other by the arms gazing face to face. They make a church, said Phim. The old and new in love.

Inspired by "Jump for Joy" by Corby Eisbacher.

Jo said, Look at that picture. Mary on the moon. It's terrible.   Ange said, Yes, you're right.   Phim said, Perhaps too ambitious.   In the upper church, Mary appeared on a round moon sailing the heavens in a dramatic tableau. Her bloodred robes billowed. Infant Jesus could not be seen distinctly. Was it a student-artist offering? The green-yellow sky was discomforting. A strange profile could be seen in the robe.   Sal said, Badness is here. They've made a corrosive picture.   Yaeli said, Wait a minute. It's poetic. Blood. Conception. Creation. The moon is her pregnancy. Struggle. Woman-force through the life-sky.

In the apse there was a more orthodox fresco. In the dome a heavenly choir of angels was gathered left and right playing musical instruments. Two angels held a decorative wreath of white flowers above the Virgin. She walks towards us out of the desert, serene and pure. She wears red, representing the earth; her blue cloak symbolizes heaven. On the walls of the church are given her five titles. Irma'am said, There she's called Help of Christians. The battle of Lepanto (1571), victory ascribed to Mary, said Ange. Joseph said, The truth is she never assists in slaughter.

After visiting the church they paused on the paved road outside, admiring the vine-covered hillside. Three men wearing strange armor were walking awkwardly towards them. They had round helmets with black visors, and large packs on their backs with four tubes projecting left and right, front and back. They had a short tube on the left arm. The grey armor appeared to be heavy-duty padding. Sal shouted, Philistia! We got action! The three men switched on, and with a dull roar began to hover above the road, moving quickly forward. One had a black mesh net in his hand.

Phim was the target, and the three moved towards him, hovering above him like dark angels. One threw the net, another kicked him, the third wrapped the net round. Then they lifted him. Meanwhile, Yaeli had dashed into the church. There was a stout wooden crozier by the altar. She grabbed it and rushed out. The three were lifting Phim out of the reach of the others, using the jets on the left arm as a weapon. Yaeli ran over, and holding the crozier leapt up and seized an ankle, hauling him down. Phim fell hard, cushioned by the net.

One of them lay on the ground. Sal tore off his armor-padding and jet-pack. The other two had moved away, and were pointing weapons. One fired. A blue flash struck the ground near Phim, still enmeshed. Shock guns, shouted Jo. Ange and Jo ran forward. They rose out of reach. There was the sound of a large helicopter. Yaeli ran forward with the crozier. Sal had stripped the man and tied him up with his shirt. He put on the pack. Jo had taken a blast to his side and was convulsing. They moved to attack Sal.

Irma gave an all-mighty high-pitched scream from behind them, throwing a stone. They turned towards her. They shot her. She crumpled up, convulsing. Yaeli leapt up again and whacked the shock-gun from his hand. Sal switched on the pack and rose above them. Phim meanwhile was still trying to get out of the mesh. It was Sal in the air against the two bad guys. Jo and Irma out of action. Ange shouted, Watch out for the helicopter. It stood directly above them, and had opened a large door. Yaeli grabbed the gun. Sal, catch this. Superb catch by Sal.

Sal rose above, and plunged down upon them. They grappled briefly, losing thrust, beginning to fall, broke free and recovered. The shock-gun was ineffective against armor. Sal flew up to look at the helicopter. It was empty apart from the pilot. They pursued. Sal plunged upon them again. They were now at 30 m. They grappled, two clouts from Sal, they broke loose. Sal struck one on the helmet. They fled into the helicopter, and it departed. Sal hovered above Phim, and raised his right arm in victory.   Thanks Sal, groaned Phim, still wrapped in the net.

Irma and Jo had recovered from being zapped. Ange had unwrapped Phim from the net. Bruised but generally undamaged. The villain, muttering and cursing, was left tied up beside the church in the shade.   Ange said, Thank you, Yaeli and Sal. We learned our lesson again. Be vigilant. Work together. Phim said, Let's walk down to the village and sit in a café.   Ein Karem was picturesque, old trees and flowering shrubs along every path. They were fighting the developers. A local led a small flock of well-groomed goats through a gate under the fig trees.

It was a climb to reach the golden domes, which they had first seen from the other side of the valley. The main church of the convent had only just been finished (2005). Monastics expelled at the beginning of the First World War; support for the convent interrupted by the Revolution. Work had resumed. It was now a jewel of the Russian Orthodox faith. The fervent spirituality of the Tsar's family in the late nineteenth century had supported foundations in the Holy Land. There had been strong feelings of connection. Russian pilgrims still continued to come in large numbers.

The Archimandrite sang the Gospel with uplifted voice. Phim could make out the words for Mary, Elizabeth and Zechariah. It must be Luke 1.39. Встав же Мария. Vstav zhe Mariya. Mary arose. Phim noticed that the icons came alive. Their eyes flickered with joy. Is this what must be? We are lifted by the beautiful voice beyond the grief of the world. We are raised above the strife in our hearts. Beyond the world's disaster. How we need to be loved for ourselves, worthless as we are. It was warm inside the voice. Russia! He felt embraced.

The Archimandrite was presiding over the silver jubilee of one of the sisters (2019). It was her hard work that had made the garden flourish and kept the compound so clean.   Restoration, building, repairing.   These thirty years have been busy years for the Russian Orthodox, she said. They painted the domes with gold. We sing the psalms every day. Our task is to meet and guide the pilgrims. Come, I will show you the holy icon Kazanskaya.   She took them to the small church. Infant Jesus stood beside Mary who wore a red veil. Holy protection for Russia, she said.

Vibrant color lit by the sunlight of the promised land – that's the point, the daylight through this color, the sons of Jacob, a rainbow lives in God's mercy forever. The speaker was a photo-journalist. He was old. Himself an artist, he'd been there when Chagall had made the windows. Phim looked at them. Naif art. A free-flow of symbols and images. Is it a map of the dreaming mind? Phim said, Sal, what do you think? Overrated. So much twentieth-century art is like this. Pure freedom paints a self-indulgent mess. Yaeli said, It's more sophisticated than you think.

Abell Synagogue, Hadassah Centre & thanks to David Rubinger.

Chagall was praised as a modernist and a Jewish artist, said Yaeli. His work focused on his boyhood in Russian-Jewish Vitebsk, a way of life destroyed by the pogroms, which drove the Jews out to America and to Israel. Praise for Chagall was partly fueled by European guilt about the persecution of Jews. Chagall himself wrote about his own experiences of this, being stopped in a pogrom, denying that he was a Jew to save his own life. His art brings back to life the Vitebsk that was lost. It's a nostalgic surrealism.

Yaeli explained, Chagall's art grew at
the interface between art and
psychology. While Freud was
interpreting dreams, Chagall and
Picasso were pouring the fragmented
modern mind onto canvas. Chagall calls
for a dream-reader. We need a key.
Consider The Green Violinist (1923-4).
They say he's Elijah, but I think he's a
Rabbi, uniting and elevating the
community by the Torah, the violin. His
greenness shows life. He dances above
the town. Rooftops are his clothes – the
heavens. He unites two houses, left and
right. Look, Irma, from him we're born.
Music and dance make communion
with God, pure Hassidism.

The guide explained, This is an active orthodox Synagogue with services every day. God lives in worship here. It's also a holy work of art.   Look how the bema, the platform, is here in the centre. It's lower than the surrounding area. You step down. Unusual. The twelve windows pour colored light upon the centre and the congregation. The ancient family is in the light of the windows. We below are the surviving children. There's a glass surface on the table, placed on a white woolen parochet, covered with Hebrew writing. See how it reflects the colors. It's an ark-covering.

A local man told them how he fell in love with Ein Karem. I love the ancient olive-trees. I was visiting with my wife once. There was a fire. A campfire was burning up an olive. We saved it. I dedicated myself there and then to caring for the olives. Week by week we treat the trees to keep them healthy. The place has improved in fifty years. Trees were planted. But they want to put in huge ugly hotels. Increase the cash flow. We're fighting to keep it a peaceful garden. There are already thousands of pilgrims every day.

As they drove towards Jerusalem, they talked about various things. Imagine, said Yaeli, that there were a penalty for eating meat. You eat a steak. You enjoy lamb or goat shish-kebabs. In penance, you have to endure the same bull bellowing in your ears, or the same lamb bleating. Maybe that would make you pause. Phim said, I like that. Hear the pitiful bleating for an hour. Surely it's true that modern abundance is immoral. There is unnecessary and wasteful consumption. Our ancestors rarely ate meat. It was very special. Jews should feel guilty, said Yaeli.

Yaeli said, Jews are told to shake four kinds of plants together in the Festival of Sukkot, remembering our salvation from Egypt. (Lev. 23:40) What's the meaning of this ancient mitzvah? The plants are willow, palm frond, myrtle and citron (called etrog). As a people, Jews are often disunited. Different cultures, different languages. Different politics, different worship. But in the gift of salvation we are one. In our suffering and growth we were one. Shake the four species together, in unity we fulfill God's command.   Phim said, That's good, Yaeli, could that also be the whole world?

With thanks to Isroel Glick "Oneness in Many" video on Chabad.org.

Phim remembered the lettuce-whirler he had at home, a device that always delighted him. A perspex bowl, with a plastic-resin colander perfectly balanced, and a lid with a plunger which fitted exactly. When you plunged it, the basket inside whirled round very fast and the lettuce released its water. It lasted for minutes, far longer than one expected, smooth and silent, on and on. He thought of the earth, an enclosed system, spinning through space, and all her complex interactions continuing for so long, one day to end, but for the length of time it was a miracle.

What do you say, Jo, asked Phim, when they question historical facts? Joseph said, We reply to this, as do all the principal faiths, with the statement that the scripture is true. But of course the truth is that history, legend and truth have walked hand in hand from the beginning. Adam and Eve. Noah and the flood. The truth is not in the historical fact but in the deeper meaning. A deeper truth. God is outside history. The concept of the God of Israel is difficult. Can you truly grasp it? Start by considering the miracle of life.

How healthy it is to be able to take criticism and improve, said Phim. But how hard. The teacher gives us a parable and we get wisdom. It works when we know what he's talking about. Allegories. Look at those monsters. Chopping up children and serving them for lunch. Well, they do exaggerate. But we do need to be better. On both sides. Don't think revenge. Think forgive. After what they did? Yes, otherwise you'll be working out your grievance for a thousand years. Shall I give examples? The teacher must teach reconciliation. We must heal anger, said Irma.

We must love one another and live, said Saleem. This should be at the beginning and end of everything we say about faith, both Christian and Muslim. The revelation of creation is granted to us. The awesome powers of science given to us. Energy and medicine we received from God. We need to rewrite the creeds. Mosque and Church and Temple side by side. The totality of information we've gained. What would this mean? Can we say that our neighbor is a demon? I love you for your goodness. God is real in my love. We have to leap upward.

God AND man, said Saleem, we always get stuck on that. Phim said, Yes, if you take it at the basic level. But if you think more deeply, it must be true. Go to the highest level. God teaches us about Himself, but his reality is not human. Yet his love is present in the whole creation. The soul is breathed into us by Him. His holy prophets are His voice. They are all God and man. JC gathers all of this into a most perfect existence. Teaching. Innocent for God, he repeats the pure sacrifice and pays for all.

Phim was thinking, As we approach Jerusalem, we need to think about the Muslim point of view. How do they feel? What do they believe and hope – and unite our love with them.   Sal, what do you feel about Jerusalem?   Don't be daft, Phim. Same as you. Holy city. The centre of ancient faith. A turning point for the whole world. We were sent here by the Holy Prophet Muhammad (pbuh). He was informed by Gabriel. The Koran is our guide-book. We know God dwells here, worshipped in holy psalms. From before and today. We belong here.

Tell us, said Phim, about Muhammad's night journey to Jerusalem. The miraculous night journey (c. 621 CE) has no obvious parallels in Judaism or Christianity, said Sal. There are various levels of understanding. The Koran Surat Al-Isra (17.1) gives a brief reference. "Glorified is God who took his servant Muhammad on a night journey to the farthest mosque." Commentators in the Hadith (books of guidance) disagree about this, but it is generally taken to be the Temple Mount, where they later built Al-Aqsa Mosque (the farthest). Angel Gabriel guides him. He flies on a mythical winged steed, called a Buraq.

The account of the night journey provoked reaction. It was a test. Was Muhammad telling the truth? Some rejected him. The faithful believed. How was it possible? With God all is possible. We have a literal wonder, and an allegory. It is a vital allegory. Night-time is the time of dream. There are holy dreams. Daniel had a dream. Gabriel came to Joseph in dream, giving him information. In the fullness of time Gabriel comes to Muhammad. He gives him the Koran. Teach the Arab nation! He brings him to Jerusalem; he gives him the knowledge of the true God.

Daniel 8.15-17; Mt 1.20; Lk 1.19.

The direction of prayer, the Qibla, said Sal, is very important in Islam, as it is for the Jews. Jerusalem was the first Qibla, and this was later changed to Mecca. Perhaps this shows Islamic confidence that it is the culmination of God's plan, surpassing all before.   Jews pray toward Jerusalem, said Yaeli. Synagogues often have a plaque to show the east. In Japan, however, they would have to face west. Christianity likewise, said Joseph, churches are built with the altar in the east. In early days they prayed in expectation of Christ's return from the east.

1 Kings 8.44-45; Daniel 6.10; Mt 24.27.

Yaeli had been teaching Phim Hebrew. He read the white letters on the blue sign. He asked her, What does the name actually mean? Yaeli said, Ah! Jo said, Keep it secret. It's holy. Phim searched his iPhone and came up with various possibilities. Foundation of peace. Dwelling of peace. Looking to peace. A Jewish site said, Feel awe before God. Saleem said, Well, obviously the root is Shalom, with another word. In Arabic it's Al-Quds. The Holy. Phim was puzzling with the Greek transliteration. Ange said, There's Holy Spirit flowing through the Greek, Phim. Yes, said Irma, Septuagint.

The holy tree, said the guide, from which the cross was made.   Phim had a sudden revelation. In the centuries of Christian rule in Palestine (c 300-640 CE), the Byzantine Church was building a pilgrim faith. Just as the Jews had done, before the loss of the Temple. Then Islam arrived and took control. Pilgrimage became difficult. Later, the new churches rejected pilgrimage and returned to the text. Islam meanwhile had become the pilgrimage faith par excellence.   Being a pilgrim confirms our faith, thought Phim. We live with the senses. We travel into the book of the Terra Sancta.

The guide explained. According to Eastern Orthodox tradition, historically the cross is connected to Abraham. The Holy Trinity appeared before him in the shape of the three angels, as shown in the famous icon. He was given three staves. Lot sinfully slept with his daughters when he was drunk. What to do? Abraham gave him the three staves (Trinity) for redemption. Plant them outside Jerusalem. Water them with the Jordan. A tree grew. Later the wood was used for the cross.   Phim was thinking. In the Ekklesia, stories join stories. Holy truths become linked. They teach God.

The guide explained. Look, there's Gabriel the archangel on the wall. You can see ancient Byzantine-style mosaics. The monastery was a lively Georgian enclave for a time, and then they sold it to the Greek Orthodox. Here's a beautiful golden throne (Orthodox). Why did they focus on the cross in this early foundation? An ancient sinful shame was transformed to glory. Truly, what was that sin? The guide, who was a monk, did not say. He only said, Saint Helen's discovery of the cross was vital to the growth of the Church.

Two brothers stood apart reading a Bible. They appeared glad to see Phim. We're from a monastery, also called Holy Cross. Benedictine Episcopal, New York. Both the brothers had shaved their heads. One was African-American. The other Hispanic-English. They were intent and purposeful. Visit us, Phim, they said, rest with us and breathe. The wind through the trees, the rain on the fields is good. We can read and pray together. They offered him a hug and he accepted. Who were these brothers appearing and why? It's nice to hug, he thought, surprised at himself.

The guide pointed, There behind the icon screen, in the holy place, is where the tree is said to have grown. There was a round silver plaque, highly polished, dated 1908. It was similar to the silver covers found on icons. On the plaque there were three trees, a Lebanon cedar, a pine and a cypress. Those must be the three staves, said Irma. It's all symbolic, said Sal. What's the meaning of the trees? That's easy, said one of the New York brothers, the Lebanon cedar was used in the Holy Temple.

Sparks fly upward from a bonfire on an autumn day. These were my favorite words for a long time (Job 5.7). Each spark is a person in the family going back ten thousand years.   I can't face going to Yad Vashem, said Phim. When I was younger I spent a lot of time studying the Holocaust and reading witness accounts. I absorbed the whole thing. It felt like my own personal trauma. It filled me with an overwhelming sorrow, so deep and dark that I thought it was not good to live. I am sorry, Yaeli.

They were walking through the old city,
a stroll to get to know Jerusalem.
There's the eighth station of the Via
Dolorosa, said Phim. They paused a
moment and bowed their heads. They
turned right at a corner which said
Ethiopian Monastery. The old city was
completely paved with Jerusalem stone.
In the Muslim section older stone was
still visible, cracked and worn. In the
Jewish section there had been refacing,
so that it looked clean and new. Most of
the alleys winding between dwellings
and religious houses were narrow. There
were frequent arches where you ducked
your head.

There were Latin crosses on the doors on the right of the alley. Arches over the alleyway. A section of column stood against the wall, making a convenient seat. Is this the Holy Sepulchre, asked Phim. There were few street-signs. It was easy to get confused. It appeared to be part of the Holy Sepulchre. They turned   right   down   another   alley. Crosses on every door. Saint Helen found the true cross somewhere around here (c 326 CE), said Joseph. It changed in meaning, said Ange, after it appeared in vision. The Church adopted it as a logo after that.

Irma said, Look, someone has put a picture of the Blessed Virgin on the wall. The doors and windows had all been painted light blue. Ange said, If there are rooms here, they are likely to be for religious. Phim put his hand on the walls as they went by. Old stones and new stones. Some appeared to be ancient. None of these buildings would have been here in this form, all have been rebuilt. Phim thought about how many generations had lived. He felt a longing to know the people, to share their lives through the ages.

Who lives in the old city now, asked
Phim.   Yaeli said, There are a handful
of old families who have hung on
through thick and thin. Sometimes
exiled and returning. People who owned
property and had a prosperous shop.
Inevitably if you're still here, someone
has asked you to be a guardian. Feelings
run strongly. Some communities are
small, like the Armenians, who know
one another personally.   In   the
nineteenth century, Jews were less than
half the number of Muslims. Jerusalem
was a small town. In the twentieth
century this was reversed. Population
grew rapidly from around 1900.

Was it fancy dress? In the narrow alley in front of them, glinting in the sun, there was a bulky man in armor with a large black shield with a white cross. Next to him was a slim figure in a robe under a steel cuirass and turban. Long curving sword. Next to them was a stocky brown man, a scar on his face, wearing Roman armor, brandishing a bright stabbing sword. The others drew their swords, a scimitar, a broad sword. Ange said, Run.   They turned and ran. The Roman was very quick, and grabbed Phim.

The Crusader and Saracen stood shoulder to shoulder and prevented Ange and Sal from breaking through. The Roman disappeared with Phim, and out of sight he opened a door, and closed it. The Crusader and Saracen then turned and ran off. Sal and Ange followed but there was no sign of Phim. Where had he been taken? Which door? Yaeli said, He's still got his mobile if they don't take it from him.   Irma shouted out, Phim!   No reply.   A Rabbi appeared walking towards them. Pray, said Yaeli, what else.   So they prayed, hoping this would not be the end.

The villains had taken off their costumes and were dressed in white cassocks with thin black belts around.   One never knows what they will look like, thought Phim, wondering how to escape. They were in a courtyard off the alleyway. Phim heard Irma call but the man hissed at him, Do not reply.   The other two lifted a hatch and revealed a spiral stairway going underground. They descended it. Soon they were deep in the rock. They came to a room with machinery. A bed inside an MRI donut containing screen and speakers.   Lie there.   They switched it on.

It was said among them that he could smell water at a considerable distance. A group moving south under pressure from the new arrivals further north who were pushing them away. A ragged herd of goats. A couple of dogs. They wore skins. Thin sunburnt faces. Long hair. One let out a cry. Excitement. The rocks here, look, in the crevice. With great effort they moved the boulders aside. Water upwelling. Under the rocks. They tasted sweet water. They were at the foot of a slope. They traced it for some distance and discovered a small stream.

Then they tightened the straps around his arms and legs. One of them said, Did you like that? This one will be a little lesson. A study of faces. You will see a few scenes. Can you draw any conclusions? Darkness came over him and he saw armed soldiers entering an ancient city. Oh they seized men and women and killed them. Pitiful cries. This was repeated with different kinds of sword, in differing costumes. Many scenes fled through his head. Look at their faces. Some were harrowed. Oh how terrible, they were elated. They were enjoying their grisly work.

Water dripped from him onto Phim's head. He was singing something softly. Up they climbed. He was carrying a small olive-oil lamp clamped in his teeth. It threw shadows onto the walls. It was a roughly-cut narrow shaft. Plenty of hand-holds. There was water some twenty metres below which sounded as Phim dislodged a small stone. On he climbed, grunting and humming. Fearful at the height Phim followed. He'd stopped. He was looking around. It was an edge. He pulled himself over. Leaving Phim in the shaft, he sprinted away through the dark city.

The king stood there wearing white robes with his head covered. He was praying loud enough for the workers to hear him. Phim was listening. He had a good voice. What is he saying, he asked himself, and it was: Blessed is God; Blessed his Name; Bless this the work of our hands O LORD, amen. There was a pause in the song where the name would be. His face was lit with fervor. The workers were setting a long stone in the sanctuary wall. The king sang and Phim thought, This is good for them to hear.

Who are they, asked one. Don't know, said another. From the East. Persian infidel, said another. Sick with dread, Phim stood behind them at the wall. They had supplies but little defense. The invaders offer peaceful terms. They open the gates. Once inside, they round up Roman soldiers and slaughter them. Phim watched them enter the Holy Sepulchre. They take the holy relics. The monks are put to death. They plunder the churches. They set flame. They've got renegades advising. They're Jews, they say. God has abandoned us. The Romans wailed at the desecration.

Phim stood apart admiring him. How handsome he was. He knew him quite well and liked him. Honor, glory, masculine pride. He was the most noble knight defender of them all. He could be ruthless to the wicked, but his love and fear of Allah was genuine. He knew that an act of mercy was pleasing to God. Allah rewards his children with blessings. He would be inwardly elated, supreme in his conceptual strength. The Franks are blockheads. They don't think. Allah grant me the victory. I will make this land peaceful for love of you. All is for God!

The stout man got off his horse and put himself at the head of the column. They entered through the Jaffa gate. Phim walked behind. The men were jubilant, marching in good order, their bush hats at a rakish angle, thin-faced and sunburnt, not one without a smile. There were local people watching. Arab Muslims and Christians, many Jews. All were joyful. Some stood silent. The General stood up and read a proclamation. "Three great religions of mankind ... the prayers and pilgrimages of devout people ... every sacred building will be protected."

An African-American dignitary and his wife at the fifth station. Phim stood in a dream. Scene changed. He was preaching. Phim listened. "The thing I thought at that moment was that it was a black man that picked it up for him and said, 'I will help you,' and took it up to Calvary. There is a desperate struggle going on. A struggle on the part of these people today to gain freedom and human dignity. One day, God will remember that it was a black man that helped His son in the most desolate moment of his life."

Adapted from "What Martin Luther King Jr. learned on a visit to Jerusalem," by Rabbi Marc Schneier, *The Times of Israel* (Jan 14, 2018).

One of them leaned over and stabbed Phim with a sharp stick. Darkness came over him again. He was walking in the streets. An ancient time. People in every kind of costume. Behind doors he listened to them. How they talked about others.   Humiliations.   Injustices. Revenges.   Cruelties.   Words   of resentment   remained   and   festered. Thorns and nettles filled the mind. Great molten hurt possessed him. It took shape.   Their fault, he said, Expend your grief on them.   Destroy them, he said, destroy. Destroy. Phim sank beneath the power of this darkness, drowning.

He lay on the floor under an ocean of darkness. He was dying. He had to rouse himself and push to the surface but he had no strength. It was too heavy. He said, I will die and that will end it. He lay there hopeless. Alone and time to die. He found a small thread of light and seized it, and pulled on it, and with utter hopelessness, still hoping he pulled, and the whole world he pulled with him, inch by inch. Dying as he strove to live, fighting to the surface. The machine shattered. He stood up.

Where am I? It was dark in the vault. An LED emitted a faint glow. He sat on the broken bed and prayed.   Far above him in the city, they were sitting in despair. Thinking of Phim, they sat together holding hands.   May God help him. Irma and Yaeli, why don't you sing, said Sal.   We'll sing together, said Ange. Jo, you start.   Om Allah.   The voices were soft and resonant, building to a powerful hum.   Irma, release your voice. I'll cry to Him with my soul, said Yaeli.   Irma took a breath and released. It was scarcely endurable.

The LED glowed brighter. Phim heard her, far away, high, clear and sharp, Irma piercing through the rock. There was a door. Through the door, a metal stairway descending. Light from beneath other doors. Subdued voices. Yaeli! Descend, Phim, there will be a way. Quickly, silently, Phim descended the stairs ever more deeply into the rock beneath the old city. It narrowed. He had gone some distance. It was pitch. The mobile! Still a few hours. A dead end. He shone the light around. Ancient blocks of stone. Someone on the stair above. He sat and asked for help.

By the stars you made, by the holy angels, by the love of all who love Jerusalem, help me O God! As he said amen, he heard them on the stair far above. It would not be long. He lay on the rough stone, and rolled on it, striking the lower blocks, which gave slightly. He pushed, they moved. A tight space. He squeezed through, replacing the blocks. A narrow tunnel. He started crawling along it, descending again. It began to curve slightly.   Is this my tomb, he thought.   Air is coming in from somewhere.   On he crawled.

Hard on the knees, thought Phim, I've only got a couple more hours of light. He paused and shone it down the tunnel. What if it ceased abruptly, and fell off into an abyss? Unlikely, he thought.   It carried on, narrow enough to crawl along, descending. He went on. He struck some brittle sticks. Bones. Powdery. Dry. Held his breath.   Rest in peace, he thought, as he crawled over the skeleton.   Am I going to join you? It'd been crawling in the opposite direction. He'd been going for half an hour.   Was it widening now?

The tunnel widened into a chamber. Phim shone the mobile. The walls had been smoothed. My goodness it's a tomb. A stone sarcophagus, oriented in the direction of the tunnel. He shone the screen. It looked like carved Hebrew.   I wish Yaeli were here! Take a picture. No! Show respect.   Deep within the rock he sang, Kadesh Kadesh God is Holy. Praise his Name, amen.   The vault came alive and crackled with power.   Phim fell to the ground, overcome by powerful emotion.   Tell no one. Live and teach.   Quickly my child, quickly.   Phim found the entrance and crawled on.

How long now? Blocks in the wall, he pushed them, they moved. Through again. Put them back. Another wall, the same again. Phim replaced them.   This is one way, isn't it?   They were slightly wedge-shaped. Close-fitting. Another wall, and as he pushed, light came in. Gingerly he pushed the stone through. It fell somewhere, tumbling down. Bright sunlight. He had to shield his eyes. Late afternoon. He pushed a couple more and poked his head through. Two metres above a paved compound. Eastern wall? Golden Gate? The handholds were good. Praying that the soldiers wouldn't shoot him, he climbed down.

It was Friday late morning. They were standing close to the Damascus Gate. Streams of worshippers were flowing through, on up towards the Dome of the Rock, to worship in the Al-Aqsa. People looked happy and chatted together. The alleys were filled with stands selling freshly baked aish (flatbread topped with olive oil and spices, thyme, salt, sesame seeds and sumac). Fasting is not required before you pray, said Sal, except during certain times, such as Ramadan. There was a young couple sharing a round piece of bread, oblivious of the people around them.

Teenagers were playing football in the Muslim quarter after the shops had closed. They kicked the ball to Phim. He trapped it, and ran with it up Al-Wad Street, pursued by the youths. One of them took the ball and ran back down the alley. Phim pursued, and kicked the ball, which rebounded from the fifth station, only to lose possession to another youth. He retook it and lifted it with his toes. Pele! Up to the roofs, clattering on the tiles. An irate face appeared around a door. The youths scattered. Phim stood, pulling his beard, feigning innocence.

Walking in the Souk El-Qattanin (Cotton Traders' Market), Phim was glad they'd spent time in Cairo. Happy the Mamluks in their prosperity (1250-1516 CE). This was said to have been the finest market in Syria. Mamluk design. The very height of modernity. A long vaulted commercial street ending in a monumental portal to the Sanctuary. A structural unity, still basically unchanged. Two bath-houses. Taxes on business became alms for God, supporting Al-Aqsa prayer or later building the Khalidi library. Phim recognized the architectural details in the Bab al-Qattanin portal. The muqarnas vaulting and the ablaq bands.

Please read *Bərešitbara* to find out about Phim in Cairo.

The long street led to the Temple Mount but only Muslims could pass through. Phim admired the high vaulted roof with skylights. The stalls were arranged left and right with goods on display. Phim's eye was caught by colorful tubs of what appeared to be assorted jelly beans and babies.   Yaeli, do you like jelly babies? Phim bought a bagful, and shared them. A boy said hello.   Where're you from? And you?   Jerusalem, my family came here with the Sheiks a thousand years ago. He was making coffee, using a gas-burner to boil water in a shiny steel drum.

He turned a tap and poured boiling water into a tall pot filled with coffee grounds. Stirred it, boiled it on the gas burner, and poured it into a silver coffeepot with lid. The aroma filled the souk. In the roof above there were patches of crumbling stone. From one of these a small piece dropped onto the tray, catapulting the coffee-pot into the air. To the boy's utter amazement, Yaeli moved instantly, grabbing it before it spilled its scalding contents onto his arm. Ouch, she said, having burnt her fingers. Sal said, That was very quick, Yaeli. Bravo.

Phim looked at the clothes hung up either side. Colorful sweat-shirts, T shirts, brand name trainers. From street to street there was a difference. The poor stalls sold cheap products. The volume of tourists differed. Phim asked a young man, Can you make a decent living? He replied in an Australian accent, We can, increasingly. We've all had instruction on how to maximize displays. If it looks good, people buy. When there's crowd-flow, gradually we clear it. It needs to be something that they can take home. Like this, Jerusalem Dome of the Rock, a painted saucer. We sell thousands.

A plush new boutique. A young woman said, We've just opened in the Arab quarter. It was called Mekhal Nougrin. Prize-winning jewelry with flower motifs (proclaimed a notice). Phim admired her Star of David medallions, Swarovski crystals and stained-glass beads, six flowers making a star. Very desirable. For Islam, she'd designed a pendant with the Arabic word Allah as a line flowing between flowers. For the Christians, a cross made of glossy black beads. These are holy items, said Irma. The young woman said, My mother Mekhal designed them to be holy. She was the daughter she said.

Inspired by the work of jewelry artist Michal Negrin.

They were selling mandolins. They also had chessboards and backgammon boards, all made of varnished wood, with the squares and spikes distinguished by different inlays. We're in this souk because rent is cheap. We're on a mission to support this quarter. We're British Muslims. I'm actually a Christian. Three men. Tidily clipped beards. One had an earring. Another was patiently smoothing the inside of a mandolin. We sell these via our patron. They were sponsored by the London Mosques, who bought the instruments and sold them in London. Made in Jerusalem. Gradually they were becoming known.

Yaeli, I want to support the poor and get something genuine. What'd be good? Yaeli said, Look at this boutique, woven baskets. Colored tiles. Small embroidered tablecloths and mats. Small carpets. Made in the Princess Centre. A workshop for people with disabilities. The quality's good, said Sal. Phim looked at another display. What on earth are these? They're called hamzas, said Yaeli. Folk protection. You hang them up to ward off the evil eye. Some of them look like a hand. Upside down they look like a mushroom. This one has a blessing for health written in Hebrew.

Inspired by Princess Basma Centre Jerusalem.

A mountainous middle-aged woman in hijab sat on the pavement in the souk with a box of strawberries. Jo, can you ask her where she's from? Speaking Arabic in a deep voice, she said, we work in a farm west of Jerusalem. We've owned this shop for three generations. I'm here on the ground to get your attention. We can't afford not to sell all these today. Phim said, How much? Irma said, A little cheaper. Can you wash them, asked Ange. They stood and ate five each. Thank you! She smiled, and showed a golden tooth.

Phim remembered visiting Harrods with his mother when he was a boy. Just the two of them.   Got Mum all to myself. It had been a tradition for a few years. Three weeks before Christmas. Early train to London. Be there when it opened. How she enjoyed looking at the glorious displays.   She isn't grumpy today.   It was an island of joy. He remembered buying the dates and dried figs and string bags of assorted nuts. A tin of Scottish shortbread (for you, dear.) Later, on the chilly porch, bashing the Brazil nuts with Dad's hammer, a perilous business.

The prosperous souk shows us a promised land, said Phim. Eden with its fruits is proffered. Milk and honey before our eyes. Sal, what's the Islamic image of Paradise? It's called Jannah, a garden. Angels will greet you with the word peace. It will be a place of palatial ease with abundant food. It's described with the puzzling phrase "gardens with rivers flowing beneath." There are rivers of water, rivers of milk. The wine is transparent, delicious without intoxication. The Koran uses metaphors, but the truth is that we cannot conceive the height of joy given to reward the righteous.

5.119; 13.23-24; 32.17; 36.56-58; 37.45-48; 56.25-26; 88.10-16.

Yaeli said, Pity the poor who cannot purchase the paradise before them. This would be torment, Phim, if you were starving. Yes, said Phim, it would be Tantalus. Sal said, That's why Islam sets such store on giving alms. Those who give to the poor will lack nothing, said Irma. Phim said, Would this kind of place be considered Mammon? I don't think so. It would be if wealth was your principal motivation, said Joseph. From ancient days, a peaceful market-place was a holy goodness. Ange said, The Lord blessed the harvest that we may better our lives.

Prov 28.27; Lk 18.22.

As they walked through the souk, gazing on the stalls, looking at the people sitting beside their wares, watching the people, Phim had a strange feeling that he was seeing the friends and acquaintances of his life walking past him. Isn't that … he thought, but they were gone before he could remember. O there's Dad, and again, there's Dad. An uncanny resemblance, the same moustache, the same eyes, but Dad never wore a turban. Another, obviously not Dad. How the heart hopes to see him. He thought about what he would have said.

Phim racked his brains. Why had Islam built the Noble Sanctuary with eight sides? He remembered the eight-sided sanctuary on Mount Gerizim, the site of the ancient Samaritan Temple. Was there continuity in faith? There were octagonal stars in the Cairo Mosques. Eight is a good number. The eighth day was the day after the Sabbath. Adam and Eve begin the journey. Also, it was the resurrection day. Two perfect squares make an octagonal star. Is it a compass-rose for the world? Our good information is not properly divisible, thought Phim, only our human error and growth made it so.

The guide book said there were eight
angels carrying the throne of God, and
there were eight gates to heaven. Phim
checked his mobile.   Eight gates to
Jerusalem.   An angel invisible on every
wall, or maybe each wall itself is an
angel.   They asked permission to go
inside.   The floor plan was an octagon
within an octagon. A circle around the
holy rock. Walk around and pray, as they
did before.   He looked at the rock.
Footstool, throne.   Angel Islam has
guarded this place for hundreds of
years.

Ps 99.5; Isaiah 66.1-2.

Phim gazed on the beauty of the Sanctuary. How well they had done! All the elements were there. The perfection of the Roman arch and dome. The glory of the Kufic script running along the walls, proclaiming word over image. Faith through the voice not by the false idol. The vegetal motifs and mathematical patterns sought to reveal the hidden messages of Allah written in his creation, a green book of secrets, or to show the heavens, a starry canopy of truth. Byzantine and Sassanian motifs were also there. The Arab is exultant in God. Look how He loves us!

Phim consulted his guidebook. Each outer wall is 20.4 m long. They match the dome's diameter and its height from the base of the drum. Why did they do that? Phim thought a moment. No domes in Egypt or Greece. Domes were the Roman gift via the arch. The early churches had domes. The heavens. The width of the world. The miracle of a perfect circle and its pi formula. It was a poetic representation of the gift of God's creation. Beneath it, the rock was left bare – the solid earth, rock for the Holy House.

Phim stared at the rock in the center. In the gentle light it seemed to show evidence that stone had been quarried. There was a cylindrical hole. Would they have put a pole there to bear a tent? This was the bedrock. There was a cave beneath used for prayer. Were the Temples placed above this? Had they cleared all the debris of ancient floors? As he gazed on the rock, he felt that letters moved there. Scratches? Chisels? Wedges? When I think not as I think I will find the peace of God.

Phim said, Tell me Sal, about Muhammad's ascent. Sal said, He ascended to heaven from this rock and returned, grace of the archangel Gabriel. It's a tradition found by hadith, and happens after the night journey to Jerusalem. The hadith state that his heart was made pure for this ascent. The details are important. They supply the truth of Muhammad's holy supremacy. He was granted a meeting with the holy prophets, an encounter with God and a vision of heaven and hell.

Phim said, The point is that God therefore grants holy revelation through Muhammad.   Sal said, Yes. He confirms the truths of Moses and Christ for the Arabs, through the Koran and through the hadith. The hadith is the Islamic version of Jewish commentary. It is very extensive, and leaps up to God from the small details. During the Miraj Muhammad receives the instruction to pray five times a day. Initially, the Lord asks for 50 daily prayers (salat). Muhammad meets Moses, and then asks God to make it easier. It's reduced to five which are said to equal fifty.

As they stood outside the Sanctuary, Phim said, I found a cartoon on my iPhone. It was cleverly produced showing the wonder of the information. Sal, the goodness of God in this poetic teaching has established the Islamic faith. Look how this has been given. It's an allegory for us to understand. The sky doors open, the height of heaven, the prophets. We must preserve the heritage of faith. The only way to do that is to teach the children. Each one claims exclusive truth. How can we keep the knowledge alive and increase our love for one another?

With ref. to IQRA Cartoon.

As he gazed on the Noble Sanctuary, which has stood on the rock for 1300 years, Phim thought, Surely this is God's will.   It was the only way to go forward. God's purpose.   Can't we say that it is, hidden from some of us. If only we could see as Heaven sees. If only we were more heavenly ourselves. If we pray with all our heart and soul, calling to Him in this place, or another place   ...   Do we really love? Why can't we be more generous to one another, puzzled Phim.

As Phim and the others walked towards the Aqsa Mosque, he remembered something. His sister calling him selfish. He was trying to write a poem. Help was needed and he didn't join in. He felt guilty but also aggrieved. It was an important verse and he had to get it right. Poetry was the whole world. The gift of art and beauty. He looked at the decoration on the dome. The surface was inlaid with beauty. An artist's hands given to the art. Total commitment. Later there were scientists. He had been selfish like that, he comforted himself.

A spasm of grief seized him as he remembered the holiday in Italy which had turned into a stay of six months. He'd learnt Italian. Why am I thinking this now here of all places? He had not understood and crumpled to the balcony floor and wept for three days. He had found a friend whom he really loved. Giacomo Benito.   He loves me, doesn't he.   Egoista!   Inexplicably, his face hard and cold, he had looked at Phim and called him selfish, and turned away. The friendship disappeared. Utterly heartbroken, he sobbed onto the tiles.

A loud aggressive roaring buzz above his head, Phim looked about and saw a commercial helicopter, painted with a pop star face, approaching the Temple Mount. The armed guards at the entrances were looking alarmed. The helicopter attempted to fly over the Dome but seemed to be encountering difficulty. It rocked from side to side and the engine tone changed. Be gone noise, said Irma. Phim was thinking the same. As if in obedience the helicopter turned away. The soldiers were ringing up their mobiles. It was quiet in the square as they approached the Aqsa Mosque.

The question was, thought Phim, where they had put the mihrab. Did it face the Noble Sanctuary (Dome of the Rock) or Mecca? It was said to date from the time of Caliph Umar's taking of Jerusalem 637 CE. Renovated and rebuilt many times. Seven great Romanesque slightly tapered arches led to seven doors on the north wall. It was impressively grand. As Phim looked back to the Noble Sanctuary above the flight of steps, the whole of the precinct appeared to be an enormous House of God, with smaller houses under the mighty sky.

Sal gave names and details at the door.
They rang up the mobiles and said OK.
Security data on individuals throughout
the region was held in vast computers.
All the police forces dovetailed together.
They bowed to Sal and Ange.   Red
carpet, said Sal.   Everyone's got their
own parking space, said Ange.   A
bright   warehouse,   with   sumptuous
chandeliers.   There   were   beautiful
marble columns in pastel blue and pink.
The roof was inlaid Lebanon cedar
beams. The dome was magnificent with
pearly white Thuluth script, and golden
flower flames ascending. Small arches
and the word of God ran round.

They stood before the mihrab installed by Saladin. White vertical stripes. Flowering mosaic patterns in the conch. Intricate foliage on the Corinthian columns. Phim thought again, Islam inherited from Greece and Rome, and displays it in the architecture. It was quiet. Early afternoon. Phim stood before the mihrab and sang out, Allah! The voice returned to him more beautifully. Sal, he said, looking around. Where? Somewhere else. Salam! The commander's tent. Phim, how many times the word peace? Elegant in a white robe with a red sash. Dear friend, an orange sherbet. Let's read holy verse in the garden.

A young Imam was singing the holy prayers as Phim spent time on his own walking around the Mosque thinking. He followed the prompting of the song, walking to the mihrab in the southeast corner and admiring the colorful marble inlay. The voice sent forth the name of God, the "l" rolled like a stream of joy, and the long "ah" extended and lifted and floated through the hall. He visited the halls beneath the Mosque. It was peaceful and cool. There was a man praying before the wall facing south.

The guide said, Regard this splendid school. The historian called it the third jewel of the Haram al-Sharif. Note the characteristic entrance, a tapered arch, a fan vault, with alternate bands of red and white. An inscription for Sultan Qaytbay. As they walked in, Phim imagined the teacher and his pupils, singing in exalted joy the unity of God. It was used for preservation of Islamic manuscripts but sadly in disrepair. How many more like this, asked Sal. The guide said, There are hundreds of ancient madrasa which require restoration.   As far away as China.

Oriel was sitting in the café reading. She was reading apocrypha in Ethiopic. The Book of Enoch. Phim watched her for a moment, completely absorbed in the text she did not hear what was going on around her. Then she felt his gaze and looked up, Hello Phim! How good to see you. They sat down and ordered cappuccinos and croissants. Oriel was going to spend a few days with them visiting the Christian sites. They talked about Galilee and Samaria. Oriel said, There's so much to learn. Let's visit the Ethiopians, Phim.

Phim stood by the Ecce Homo arch imagining the scene. They were sweating profusely as they carried stretcher-loads of stone and earth up the long ramp, under which Phim now stood. They were dressed in brown cloth, tied round the waist. Stocky, grim men. They were raising the ramp towards what looked like a fortress. There were men on the walls. The work progressed. A group of archers let fly an arrow. They were gaunt. On the ground near him, wearing a red cloak, a Roman officer appeared. He shouted at them. Aqua! Rest!

They walked a little further down the street. An inscription on the wall. Look at this, said Irma. Phim paused. Just ahead of him an arrow struck the wall with a metallic ring, pocking the limestone. A grey shaft with a steel head. Ange said, Someone's got a bow. Watch out. Whish another arrow struck the wall, not far from Phim's head. Move to the other side. He's over there. They stood on the other side of the street. Phim picked up the arrow. It may be poisoned, said Jo. A light-weight carbon alloy. Phim held it and thought.

Irma, Yaeli, Sal. Let's pray together. I'll hold the arrow. Let the arrow return to the arm who released it. Phim concentrated with more effort than usual, angered by the near-miss, angered by their relentless pursuit. In his hands the carbon-shaft of the arrow began to heat up, until it became almost too hot to hold. Phim said, Let the aggression return to its home. There was a shout from the roof above them. Ange looked. A woman appeared with an arrow in her shoulder. She was trying to fix another in her leg. Phim, said Jo, Enough.

Oriel said, The first split, Chalcedon 451. The south held to the single unified nature of Christ, containing both divine and human, mysteriously unified in one, Christ consubstantial with the Father. In him, divinity and humanity are inextricably intermingled and indivisible. God shows the holiness of his presence in the humanity of his Son. Consider the transfiguration. The north chose the two natures of Christ, yoked together but separate, the pure ineffable holiness and the Adam earth. Original sin cannot mingle with God.   Phim said, Christological beauty. I find truth in both explanations.

The guide opened the door, and they were on the roof. It was a small enclosed courtyard. Phim put on his sunglasses. Beneath them was Saint Helena's chapel. There were small dwellings for monks. In a walled-off section there were trees. How did they get there, thought Phim. The dome of the sky was pale blue, and there were a few wisps of cloud.   There were   other   tourists   visiting   who reminded Phim of his family.   He felt a strong urge to lie down on the stone pavement completely naked and let the sun warm him for a minute.

Phim gently pushed the door open. There was a prayer service. Chanting at the altar. The small nave was filled with white-robed figures. A heady smell of incense. The chandelier was very bright. Phim gazed on the icon of Christ on cross. Paneling of mother of pearl inlay as they'd seen in the Hanging Church in Alexandria. Icon of the Blessed Virgin beneath the larger icon of the cross. Beautiful mother. Two women stood apart, leaning on the white wall, faces riven. Phim waited there, absorbing the surge that swelled within the room. He could almost touch it.

In a small room not far from the rooftop
monastery, there was lecture being given
by Dawid Jacob, an expert on the
Ethiopian Church.   Hello, cried Oriel.
He saw her and beamed. They gave
each other a familiar hug.   Phim, said
Oriel, this is the man you should meet.
He will explain connections between the
African Orthodox and the Jews.   He
looked splendid. A rabbi of an ancient
day. A blue velvet turban edged with
gold. His dark eyes glittered with joy.
Phim, he said, let me kiss you. Peace, he
said, and kissed Phim's beard, left and
right.

Inspired by lecture given by Ephraim Isaac at the Library of Congress.

In Jerusalem the Ethiopian presence, said Dawid, is deep-rooted. The early Biblical languages: the Hebrew source, and translations in Coptic, Ge'ez, Greek, Latin, Syriac (Peshitta) and Aramaic (same as Syriac).   In Ge'ez Ethiopia preserved one apocryphal book better than anywhere else. Enoch. Consider the resurrection of the dead. We pray this in the Amidah prayer (Gevurot). It's a central Jewish and Christian belief. It's taught by the Book of Enoch. Ge'ez preserved this the best. Become wise, Phim, sit with the learned in the courts of heaven. Deeper and better reading will save us.

See Bk of Enoch 1 ch. 51; see Job 19.25-27.

Dawid, said Phim, teach me happy in those Biblical languages.   He smiled, I can help you in your task. You need harmony models. We're a society with a long history of mutual forbearance and respect. We had Jews with us. Muslims in our nation have built churches; and Christians have built Mosques. We remember the essential truth. We are children of the same father. Brothers and sisters. Why should we war? Someone asks, Why were revelations given at different times?   We reply, The Father knows. Would the Father object if we prayed together? Look to Ethiopia and learn!

Dawid said, Let me introduce my august companion, in Jerusalem incognito for the Ethiopia Festival. An Ethiopian prince, a grandson of Emperor Haile Selassie. A tall elegant man, with a shining forehead, who could have been a hospital president or a helicopter pilot, bowed to Phim. I heard about your task from Oriel. Science and historical scholarship, when we apply them to the Bible and to Faith, will take away the mystery; and yet the need remains to unify the core of faith with the truths of modern knowledge. An impossibility? Nothing is impossible, one step at a time.

Inspired by talk given by Prince Ermias Sahle-Selassie at the Library of Congress.

Holy kings and the Ethiopian line of faith, said Dawid. They called him the King because he was the Messiah. As Solomon was. He was holy and wise and strong for the people, a savior. Here is Prince Hermiah, Phim. His family line holds the same promise, elected to stand for the people before God, reaching back to the dawn of faith. The Prince said, We descend from Solomon's son with Queen Sheba, Menelik I. Symbolically perhaps, a living icon, I am the "son of David." Our holy duty is kingship. We defend the faith and save the people.

Dawid had been organizing a three-day Ethiopia Festival. There's a concert, he said, old and new together. They stood at the back. A pop group dancing as they played. The young man undulated suggestively. They reminded Phim of 60s stars. Is that Elvis? Is that Jagger pouting? Long-haired Joni and Joan? An Ethiopian Nana? Is that Bob growling? Paul, is that you warbling?   Phim was taken by the youthful allure.   Dawid said, I don't like the music, but I would if I were their age.   Youth.   It's an eternal song. It's good for the present. Very good, said Yaeli.

It turned out that the Prince was good at playing the krar, a traditional Ethiopian harp with six-strings. He sat on a chair, strumming the chords and began to wail a psalm in Ge'ez. Was that the word Dawid said, thought Phim. Was it the same as Hebrew and Arabic? Psalm 1. Happy is the man. You love the Torah. Judgement day is the time of harvest. The grain is separated from the chaff. The wind will take it away. His voice rose; the krar beat a joyful rhythm. The song grew. Be a tree planted by water.

Inspired by Krar Collective.

He's called an Azmari, which means
minstrel, said the Prince.   He was
bowing a long-necked one-stringed
fiddle with a square-shaped sound box.
It's called a masinko. The Azmari sang
with quavering voice, enjoying his song.
Yaeli asked, How old are these
instruments?   Dawid said, Ancient.
You can find similar instruments and
variants from Aswan to Dar es Salaam.
Even in China. Technology travels when
it makes you happy.   There was a roar
of laughter.   What's the joke, asked Sal.
The Prince smiled. Hard to translate.
He rolled his eyes and did a little shake.

The festival concluded with a set by a famous Jamaican band. They were singing some old Bob Marley numbers. One Love. A new Rasta-Orthodox Church had sprung up in Kingston and London. They'd taken up Rastafarian ideas, especially the music, but otherwise had moved to an Orthodox Liturgy. The revolutionary aspect was that only women were priests, and the band was all-women. They also sang Gospel. The lead singer looked stunning. She had cropped curly hair and a mighty voice. The audience were all dancing. Both Dawid and the Prince were frowning, but Phim found himself irresistibly drawn.

Phim was thinking, round we go and round we go, a prayer for a circuit. It was a modern interpretation of ancient Ethiopian church structure, influenced by the Byzantine rotundas, and shown in the Dome of the Rock. The Holy of Holies stood at the centre. Procession and prayer was the life of the ancient Jew and continued by Ethiopia. Here is the answer, surely, as we orbit the source of life, as the moon goes round mother earth: for as long as we go round, we offer up a sacrifice of praise.

We were stubborn, said the monk, from under his black peaked hood, that's why we're still here. Armenia was the first Christian nation (301 CE). We preserve ancient liturgy from the early days. In a way, we complement Ethiopia in the south, both of us survivors, both of us deep-rooted in Jerusalem. The priest wore red and gold sleeves when he upheld the Gospel. They were singing the Creed in Armenian. Deep voices drove the shadows from the mind. Phim observed the bishop's staff, the double serpent sang to the cross, the tongues flickered like flame.

Amen Hayr Soorp   The voice trilled and fluted the phrases into the roof of the ancient church, the line of song turning and looping above their heads. The voice climbed to God again and again, calling him into the church, Holy Spirit, come to our souls with thy peace. The voice was supple and rich, an easeful melodic resonance that filled Saint James with peace.   What is she saying, asked Phim.   Oriel said, Hayr is father, Soorp is holy. Blessings be to Father, Son and Holy Spirit. It's sung during the reception of the Eucharist.

Inspired by the singing of Isabel Bayrakdarian & Armenia Sarkissian.

Blue tiles clad the pillars up to the height of a man. An indigo blue design on white. Four tiles together formed a pattern, making a flower in the centre, and four flowers, or leaves, or perhaps honey bees. You could see a cross. In ancient days the tiles were in great demand, clothing the bare stone, cool and pure. Above them on both pillars there were icons of the Blessed Virgin. Look, said Irma, you can find other patterns in the tiles. There were expensive carpets on the floor, filled with color. It was a comfortable space.

The Alexander Nevsky Church was not open to the public. It stood adjacent to the Holy Sepulchre, a plot of land purchased by the Russians to build a hospice for pilgrims, but excavations revealed important early information, and the site remains an archaeological area turned into a Church, with a beautiful iconostasis. Phim said, This is perfect. We have the feeling of praying close to the actual columns and arches put up by Hadrian. There are the steps of Constantine's first Church of Resurrection. Quietly Christ hung on the cross – showing the world what we do to one another.

Up the 177 spiral stairs to the bell-tower.
360 degree view of Jerusalem.   At last I
begin to grasp the shape of this city,
said Phim. Look, there's Mount Zion.
Who could be worthy enough to be here,
asked Yaeli. We are looking on the site
of the Holy of Holies.   Sal said, May we
look on the Holy City in peace.   They
sat in the chaste nave. Someone
sounded the organ. The Fugue in D
Minor thundered and rolled to God's
glory. Phim glanced at the Lamb and
Flag on the door, and saw him skip for
joy.

J.S. Bach. Toccata & Fugue D Minor BWV 565. Karl Richter.

Irma said, I'd like to visit the Mary
Houses of Jerusalem before we leave.
Joseph said, Let's make it a pilgrimage.
Start with Station Four, Our Lady of the
Spasm (1881). Written above the door
in Armenian and Latin   tuam ipsius
animam pertransiet gladius,   spoken to
Mary by Simon, the old priest (Lk 2.35).
Phim said, A mother suffers to raise her
child. How much would a mother feel
for him, in such an ordeal?   Irma said,
There's a cross to endure in the body,
and a cross to endure in the mind.

A cool chaste temple in Jerusalem stone. Phim thought about his mother. There she sat sowing tiny labels with red thread to be attached to his clothes. His name. He was sent away to school. Everything had to be labelled. It took hours. She looked at him and smiled. He remembered again.   Long ago. How much fun it'd been to have her to himself.   You're special to me, Phim, she'd say.   Carried away to prison, heartbroken, look at the little labels. Weep on the hard bed. Good for you. Grow up. She'd wept also.

Approaching the church entrance a pleasant garden on the right. Mary was born here? asked Phim. According to the Protoevangelium of James, said Joseph. Her parents Joachim and Anna were childless. Joachim was a rich man with abundant flocks. They were chosen for the conception of Mary without sin, as Rome teaches. The dogma of the Immaculate Conception. This was a theological assumption that grew within the Latin Church as the love for Mary grew. It elevates her close to her son, as a co-redemptrix. The Copts do not follow it but I personally find it holy.

Phim said, I've just read the Protoevangelium of James, describing Mary's birth and marriage. In Luke, Mary says, "the mighty one has magnified me." An allegory saying, I am Holy Church. In the Protoevangelium the phrase "magnify my soul" is used twice, which suggests that the author was familiar with Luke. Mary is a gift to the childless Joachim and Anna. They dedicate her to God. She lives in the temple until she is twelve. Does she somehow symbolize the soul? At the end of chapter seven, she dances on the altar steps.

There was a woman singing in the middle of the nave. He restoreth my soul. She sang with feeling. Her face showed sorrow. Her singing was painful to hear, definitely not meant to be videoclipped on somebody's phone. Phim was moved. An echo entered his soul and he felt the strength of her faith. He looked at Irma. She was affected to tears. Sal also. Yaeli? She knew the words and said them along with her. She got stronger and brightened up as she sang. They stood and waited as she sang the psalm to the end.

Crusader façade, Romanesque arch,
supported by slender Corinthian
columns. Phim was surprised to find a
staircase descending deep into the rock.
Phim said, An old rhyme – tomb, womb.
A strange truth, said Oriel.   Her soul is
born to heaven, said Irma.   Birth, said
Yaeli, and the large hollow space spoke
back, *Earth*.   Oriel said, The Blessed
Virgin gathers many meanings. We are
born from the Mother; we sleep in her at
the end.   Sal said, Isn't that going too
far?   Is that really Mary? said Joseph.
Ange said, Our bodies are recycled, our
souls stand with her in heaven.

There was a forest of ornate lamps hung throughout the shrine. A guide pointed to a mihrab. It had been used as a mosque by Islam. Phim remembered the holy tombs of Cairo. What better place to pray than before the holy remains of the mighty faithful. A Russian priest was singing. Bogoroditse (Theotokos) and spasiba (thank you). Mary looked out from the jewelled icon shielded with silver. A Russian woman, her face showing strong emotion, looked to Mary and prayed. Light gleamed on the smooth stone steps as they climbed upwards to the bright door.

Ange pointed to the medallion of Mary Magdalene above the door. Unusual to see her depicted in white. Oriel commented, She's beautiful, isn't she? The Russian nineteenth century icons marry western realism to eastern spirituality. Irma said abruptly, Grief and its healing are at the heart of faith. There's a Franciscan chapel in the Holy Sepulchre. Mary Magdalene meets Jesus in the garden. Both she and Mary were feeling bitter grief. Joseph said, Yes, indeed. John chapter twenty is a gift. Ange said, She thought he was the gardener. How could she fail to recognize him?

John 20.1-18.

From somewhere painful gusts of sorrow broke through and Phim rocked from side to side, standing by the tomb of Elisabeth Feodorovna (1864-1918), his tears falling. He felt that he should fall to the floor in abandonment but he could not really understand why. What was this sorrow? The others had not noticed. Pull yourself together, Phim. Trembling he read the bio on the tomb.

There was a visit by Prince William, Duke of Cambridge. Security herded them aside. The Prince appeared, his bald head shining pink in the sun. He looked at Irma and smiled. Archimandrite Roman, all in black, led him to the door, and a sister offered him bread and salt. Welcome to our convent. The Prince looked pleased. Later, Phim found a videoclip. He had come to offer flowers at the tomb of Princess Alice of Battenberg, his great-grandmother (1885-1969). Prince William stood with bowed head, honoring her memory.

Irma said, This place is a comfort. Joseph said, The Blessed Virgin departs peacefully from her fleshly tabernacle. Her son stands above her in bright spirit gathering her soul to heaven.   Ange said, In past ages, to be granted a peaceful departure, unplagued by disease or disaster, was a blessed gift. Oriel said, If we go back to the roots of faith, we discover that faith itself was our only weapon against death.   Has that changed today, asked Sal.   Yaeli said, A crux or a crutch? It must be a book.

I like that gentle mosaic icon, said Ange, pointing to the apse of the main church. It was Mary with infant Christ. Gold ground, and golden highlights. She looks to him, holding him on her left hand. Her right hand at her stomach gestures to him, offering him to us. Wavy lines symbolize the sea. His sandals upon the top line. His eyes upon us. His right hand blesses, placed beneath his mother's throat. Above, the abbreviated Greek phrase "Mother of God" (Mītīr Theou MP ΘΥ). His left hand holds an open bible. I am the light of the world.

They'd started 50 years earlier, an outreach to the Jerusalem poor. It had become an old people's home looking after sisters and others from the community. There were even two Muslims, who had grown up with some of the others, and been allowed in on the basis of friendship. A couple of young volunteers were helping. Many were in wheelchairs. It survived on donations. The Palestinian cook (Muslim) had to go through a checkpoint and it was an office of love and patience since it took a couple of hours every day. He is so good, said a sister.

The sister showed them the day room where the elderly rested. Some required help to move about. A volunteer had come from France. My year before university. I chose to work in homes in Israel. This one (Notre Dame) for a few months, then one in Bethlehem run by the Order of Malta.   They were having a fête. One of the senior sisters had a tambourine. She sang joyfully. The residents grew lively. The volunteer started dancing. Irma pushed a wheelchair around the room. Phim took hands with an elderly resident and led her gently about.

Phim found a videoclip on his iPhone about the Holy Sepulchre. Pope Francis and Patriarch Bartholomew knelt and kissed the slab.   What a fine forehead, thought Phim.   Bartholomew had removed his black hat, revealing a shiny pate. A long curly lambs-wool beard.   A Bishop intoned in Greek, subtitled, *For the peace of the whole world.*   Francis and Bartholomew stood together wearing white and black.   *We affirm the truth of the Scriptures.*   There was a black Madonna (Greek).   She gazed on them as they knelt and prayed.   She looked at Phim from the tiny screen.   *He is risen.*   She looked happy.

Patriarch Bartholomew & Pope Francis, Church of the Holy Sepulchre, 20140525.

Oriel pointed to a lamp hung against the wall of the aedicule.   Beauty is the way. It was a long-life candle with a yellow flame. There was a red glass guard around it. Three chains went up to a round porcelain ornament with interfolded wings that looked Chinese. Phim thought, China!   At university he had longed to become fluent and read the old masters. A Jesuit priest had told him once that he'd glimpsed the Lord through the beautiful calligraphy. He wears disguises, he said.

The guide sketched the archaeology of the site. It was confusing. He pointed to the large square limestone blocks. This was part of the platform on which Hadrian built the pagan temple. It was said to be for Venus. (There was another on the Temple Mount for Jupiter.) Saint Helena ordered its destruction. Search for the holy cross. Relics were found in a cistern deep under the rubble. No coincidence there. God told us what the pagan temple was. It was a death to God – abomination and desecration. God returns to life in the house they raise.

What sudden thoughts assailed him. Impassioned imaginings gripped his mind. A scenario grew from an encounter with a woman they'd met. How insistent it was. STOP! He shouted within the mind. No good. The thoughts returned, more interesting than before, a story developed. He wondered STOP! He looked to the tomb. Call His beautiful Name. He intoned the Name silently in five languages. At His Name heaven will bow. As he gazed on the tomb, there was a sense of relief. The troublesome thinking faded.

Phim remembered a program he'd seen once about the shape of the cross. They explained why the Romans favored it. It was grim. It was likely that they used various kinds. Up the stone steps to Golgotha. Irma placed her foot where the step was deeply worn. Each one stumbled as they walked to the stations. This was where he was crucified. He hung there in bright lights and gold. There was a group of solemn Sikhs who stood quietly.   A sister in black, a sister in white, in tears.   Where are you, Phim heard himself cry.

If you put your head on the altar placed above the column to which Jesus was tied during the flagellation, you would hear laughter. Phim put his head on the altar. Nothing. Wait. He could hear something. Quiet at first. Soft gentle whispering that made no sense. Gradually he could hear phrases. Information. Stories about wars. Fearful tales about marauding gangs. The violence suffered by women. The destruction of places you loved. The development of new military weapons. Poison gas drifted on the Somme and he heard his grandfather gagging.

As they descended the steps in St Helena's chapel to the place of the finding of the holy cross, Phim ran his fingers on the crosses scored on the wall, put there by countless medieval pilgrims. Were these sins? Voices of unnumbered billions, sufferings endured, the leper beseeching the Lord for healing, the miner working the seam for gold. Victoria's grief for Albert. Steps descending and ascending. A long walk for the human race to arrive a place where all can read. His bones creaking, thank God for his hands in the hospital today, thought Phim.

Male voices filled the Sepulchre as the Armenians processed down to the chapel of the finding of the cross. They formed a circle around the protodeacon, who wore a crown-like mitre, and over his left shoulder a long red orarion embroidered with gold crosses. They climbed the stairs up to Saint Helena's chapel and lined up within the altar rails. Phim stood by the stairs, marveling at the beauty of the chapel, the abundant lamps all lit and burning. The singers appeared to be heavenly spirits gathered in a room of holy flame.

Oriel said, When you have a monolithic system, without critics who have the power to bite, the system inevitably corrupts and fails. One sure history lesson. Martin the best Catholic biter, then followed the renewing saints, rivalry, struggle, mortars and medicine. Clever boys build their own team. We get wars. Technology became astral. Evaporate a nation in a flash. How can we remain healthy and uncorrupt, without apocalypse? Yaeli said, We need to bite one another without taking life. Struggle to defeat − improve − one another without malice. We have to be friends. We need to trust and love.

It was a Coptic liturgy. Their heads were covered with black hoods studded with stars. The Coptic Chapel stood at the far end of the aedicule, a Romanesque arch, with a decorative iron grill. There was a large icon of Christ on it, triumphant and serene. A red cape flew behind him in the golden aureole, his wounded right hand held out. Inside there was a Greek icon of the Virgin and trays of long candles and bottles of incense. In the ever-new enactment of the Gospel truth, the Copts were showing the resurrected Lord.

A priest was intoning Coptic liturgy.
Look up there, said Sal.   Phim looked
at the dome. It looked like a flower or a
sun. A window of sky in the centre.
Millennium celebration. The tomb stood
directly beneath. From the side window
came a shaft of light through the clouds
of incense. Lines of poetry he'd studied
long ago. Light visible. Creation is never
without pain. Was that Dante or Milton?
The fingers of light visible. A bright pool
on the floor. A sacred gift – they rejoiced
in the old Temple, someone had told
him.

Jn 1.1-5; T. S. Eliot, Choruses from The Rock IX (1934).

Friday evening, the siren sounded joyfully over the hills.   Yaeli said, Let's join them at the Wall.   They followed the crowds and stood on the stairs of St Mary of the Germans, viewing the plaza. Close by, there was a large circle of men and women. Men wearing skull caps. Women loose hair. Couples danced inside the ring. Next to the Wall, a circle of men of all ages, some Hassidic. A table with Torah. Yai! Yai! Yai! they chanted, jostling one another.   They look so happy, thought Phim, wishing that he could join them.

On the approach to the Western Wall they had to separate. Officially, it was a synagogue. Women to the right, men to the left. We are not allowed to pray together, said Yaeli. For a liberal Jewish woman, it's difficult. Inevitably women are placed lower. We still have something like this among the Copts, said Irma. Sal said, This is the dividing line between advanced faith, and the gender-walls of ancient days. It's given to focus thought on prayer, said Phim, and not on your neighbor's wife (or husband). But times change.

Phim was reading the pamphlet. Jews prayed at the Western Wall because they could not pray in the old Temple precinct. The rabbis asserted that God's presence had never departed from the Holy of Holies, possibly sited where the Dome of the Rock now stood. First built by Solomon, rebuilt after the Babylonian destruction, restored by Herod, destroyed by Rome. The western perimeter wall survived. It was a massive wall with deep foundations. A wonder. Phim looked at the wall. There is glory in this open wall. Perhaps that's the point. All ye nations! God is here.

Pss 22.27; 67.2; 117.1.

There was a pale young man of average height wearing a black hat, with a lock of curling hair hanging down, with his face close to the wall, his left palm on the wall, and his right hand held the book. He was completely absorbed in his prayer. His head and body rocked forward and back, and his lips were moving. You could see his bony shoulders through the black jacket. Phim couldn't hear the words, but he felt a surge of spirit. He trembled at the intensity, and wanted to embrace the young man.

What do you call the blanket he's wearing, asked Phim. It's not a blanket, it's a prayer shawl, said Yaeli. It's called a tallit. There was a man at the wall pulling the tallit over his head. It had black and white stripes, with white tassles, and knotted cords at the corners. Those fringes are called tzitzit, said Yaeli. The question is whether Jesus wore one or not, said Joseph. Did the woman grab the tzitzit? Phim was admiring the blanket and thinking he wanted one. So that's the Torah, isn't it, he said. A portable tent, said Yaeli.

What's that he's got on his head, asked Phim.   The man had a small black box strapped to his forehead, the strap went round his head. He had another black strap on his left arm, secured around the biceps and spiraling round the forearm to the fingers.   Holy verses on parchment, said Yaeli, it's a visual reminder to him and his family to put the Torah into the memory, and to think upon it. It was that that gave the Jews their great advantage. Their best people trained mind and memory from childhood. Book-learning is the way of God.

There was a group of Jewish men at the entrance, dressed in suits with kippah (skull-cap), carrying a large silver cylinder more than a metre long, an ark of the scroll.   They walked towards Phim and the others and stopped at a table with an umbrella. There were six of them. They opened the ark and took out a loudhailer, and a black box, which looked like a battery power-unit with a cable. They plugged in the loudhailer and pointed it at Phim. He felt a sonic blast, ear-splittingly loud. He grasped his head and stumbled forward.

What's wrong, Phim, called out Yaeli from across the square. He couldn't speak. The man was trying to blast him again but Phim had moved closer to the wall, and was hidden by someone praying. Yaeli had seen what was happening and started running towards the men. She pushed into the men's section, pursued by security. The six men were waiting and threw her violently aside. Security grabbed her. The man blasted Phim again, and missed, striking the wall. Everything went silent, a high voice cried out in prayer. He blasted again, striking one of the caper bushes, which shattered.

A loud noise was heard, like a great congregation shouting, and it seemed as though the wall itself wavered, sending back a reply to the man with the weapon. What was it? It struck him hard and he crumpled. The loudhailer in his hand split in two. The other five now started to leave, but security had realized that something was wrong, and seized them and their equipment. They struggled violently but the security men were well-trained. They let Yaeli go and she ran to help Phim. Phim stood up, and looked around. What was that, he said.

Sal looked at the weapon, and said, This is a sophisticated close-quarter anti-personnel device. If it hits you full-force on the head, it can kill you. It destroys eardrums and can also affect the eyes. Military forces agreed not to use them. Illegal. I was lucky again, said Phim. Are you OK then, asked Irma, from the barrier. Feel all right, let's spend time at the wall. Separated but close enough, heads covered, they stood by the wall. Phim placed his hand there and prayed. The stone was warm. Home, he thought.

Yaeli said, The dream of building the Third Temple remains, but gradually the Wall has grown into the life of the faith.   Is it better this way? asked Phim. No Jew would say that, but there's something deeply satisfying here. Look at it. Feel its power. A simple wall. Jerusalem sky.   Pray, my children. I am with you in prayer in this holy place and at any wall in any place on earth, when you stand in peace and call to me. Face any wall and face to me, anywhere on earth.   Sal said, That is beautiful.

As they walked away from the Wall, there were crowds milling. Not far from the Burnt House, Phim noticed a man with a walking stick. As they moved towards the Sephardi Synagogues, he felt a needle strike his left arm. A small round bobbin with a feather hung from his shirt.   Sal, I've been hit by something.   As Phim turned, he felt a projectile whip past his ear, and strike the stone wall. The man lowered his walking stick and hastened away. Ange had noted him, but there were too many people.   Phim had started to groan.

Sal gently pulled away the dart and then tore off Phim's shirt. Already the skin had discolored. Phim was reeling about groaning. Sal was looking worried. It's a poison. We must get him to a hospital. Yaeli! Yaeli walked over to the soldier and spoke rapidly in Hebrew. The soldier radioed for help. Two women soldiers appeared. Phim was retching and falling over. The soldiers took them to a nearby military clinic. Sal now looked desperate. Irma, said Ange, start praying. This looks serious. Irma started singing the Omm Allah. Phim was blacking out. The soldiers led him inside.

Yaeli showed the dart and explained the situation.   Phim had lost consciousness. They checked his pulse. They checked his eyes.   No brain damage yet, said the woman doctor. We don't know what this poison is, but there's something we can do. They checked Phim's blood type, rhesus alpha, and rapidly set up a blood flow transfusion.   The doctor said, This will clean the whole bloodstream and remove the poison. I only hope there's been no damage. They took a sample for testing. Phim lay there, his face grey, and the blood flowed through.

As Phim lay on the bed after the transfusion, they returned with the sample. It appears to be an unknown poison, perhaps nerve or brain-damaging. Phim, tell us how you felt. Phim said, I felt terrible. Burning sensation in the arm, numbness, nausea, then the brain function started to go, couldn't make sense of anything, eyes started to go dark, couldn't stand, and can't remember any more. How do you feel now? Feel great. We'll do some tests just to make sure. Phim said, Thanks, I think you saved me. Sal said, I'm sure they did.

Up the narrow stairway to the top of the walls. It was a bright sunny day. They emerged into a small stone courtyard. It had been recently restored. There were metal stairs and walkways that led along the walls north and south. From one of these, a burly red-faced and silver-bearded figure descended, and looked at Phim and shouted OH HO! He walked over, and with a wrestler's agility grabbed Phim and lifted him up high. Put him down, shouted Sal, but the man had moved very quickly to the metal stair.

Kindly let me go, said Phim. What are you trying to do?   The silver-beard grunted but said nothing.   Is it money? I can offer you a hundred dollars.   The man ignored him.   Perhaps that's cheap.   How about two hundred and fifty?   The man was now standing above the Jaffa Gate, in full view of the people below, and said, Prepare to meet your maker, you miserable sin-crusted worm, and with a great grunt he threw Phim out into the air about the square. Is this it, thought Phim, and with utmost speed said, Thank you God.

Providence however had not forgotten him. From out the Jaffa Gate trundled a small white van, hauling a red load in a deep plastic barrow. There'd been a consignment of best quality Neapolitan tomatoes, and they'd been overlooked in a corner of one of the souks. It had been necessary to load them up, a messy job, since they'd become very soft. They now received Phim with a loud squelch. Welcome! Am I saved, he thought, to drown in a rotten tomato? He saw Irma in the sky, looking over the edge, calling out, Phim, are you all right?

Phim was undamaged by the fall. After cleaning up, they returned to their walk. You could walk around almost the entire city on the walls.   Yaeli said, Let's sing a psalm as we go round. Start with this: The Lord loves.   The gates of daughter Zion, added Ange.   Count her towers, said Joseph.   Pray for her peace, said Sal.   May the Lord bless you from her, said Phim.   In the midst of her, praise the Lord, said Irma.   The word of the Lord from her, said Oriel.   Blessed be the Lord, who dwells in Zion, said Yaeli, amen.

Pss 9.14; 48.12; 116.19; 122.6; 128.5; 135.21; Is 2.3.

With permission they stood at the back of the synagogue as the young men sang out a psalm of peace. All dressed in white, with white kippah (skull cap). Later they climbed to the inner balcony within the dome; and then outside, walked around the outer balcony, with a 360 degree view of the city. The design was from the nineteenth century. A perfect house for God, said Phim, the square and dome. The synagogue echoed Byzantine Church and Mosque. The ark was baroque, with the ten commandments lettered in gold Hebrew. A gold crown, who was that for?

They stood in Hurva Square. Yaeli said, Here's the synagogue founded by Rambam when he was briefly in Jerusalem. A column stood outside. A page of his wisdom on the wall. It was a two-aisled hall with columns. A Rabbi had just finished expounding Torah. It had been refloored long ago and the columns were half-buried. Phim was intrigued. Was that a Crusader roof? He read the guide. Maimonides wrote to his son from Jerusalem, We found a ruined house with columns and made a synagogue (1267). It was used for about 300 years (closed 1599).

As they sat in the café, the owner mentioned that there was a light festival that evening. They project images onto the Synagogue. It's amazing.   They waited until it started at 9 pm. A video-projector played a film on the synagogue wall. Light-lines sketched the shape. A globe of cascading stars turned into blocks of stone. The image melted to show inside the building. Glittering chandeliers. The wall built up again. An ornate veil was whisked away to reveal a tapestry of flowers. Mighty doors swung open to show a library with ancient scrolls.

Inspired by Solaris Light Festival 2017.

Compare the picture of the burnt-out shell with the present beauty, said the guide. What had this been? The architecture gives you clues. The ceilings are like crusader churches. The Aron Kodesh stands within two gothic windows. It could have been an icon screen with saints. There's blue sky above, with Hebrew letters, where Christ would be blessing in a Greek Church. The guide pointed to a column outside and talked about Mecca.   Had a church and a mosque and a synagogue played musical chairs?   Natural light filled the house. Delicate ironwork guarded the Bimah. It's peaceful here, said Phim.

Crowds milling in the Jewish Quarter. Jews of all sorts and other tourists. Phim noticed the hair of three young women, a light blond shoulder-length, softly catching the sunlight; another, a torrent of glossy black curls; another, a rich chestnut brown, gathered in a dancing ponytail. How the world had changed on hair, the religious guidance and modern customs. He felt his beard. Rough, perhaps unpleasant to look on. His head had not seen the shampoo for a few weeks. He sniffed. Probably OK. Natural body oils healthy. Three hijabs walked by and he thought, They look nice.

They found a café run by Ottolunghi and Tamim, two famous TV chefs. Ottolunghi had Jewish background. Tamim was Arab. They had partnered together to produce a famous book of recipes. Both communities, they said, share the same cuisine. Different versions of the same thing, said Yaeli. Sal said, Ethnic blending in cuisine. What shall we have, asked Phim. Babies, said Yaeli, laughing. Irma said, By whom? I like the idea of multicultural kids, mixing is healthy, said Phim. Well then, said Yaeli. Are you serious, said Phim. Irma felt a pang.

Inspired by Yolam Ottolenghi & Sami Tamimi cookbook Jerusalem.

Phim said, What are you making? The chef said, My tomato and pomegranate salad. Take your fresh tomatoes, dice them, small jewels. The same with red onion. Red pepper. Pomegranate seeds. Crushed garlic, white wine vinegar, pomegranate molasses, olive oil. Ground all spice. Salt. Mix and pour over the salad. Oregano, earthy and green. It looks beautiful, said Phim. This is popular, said the chef. Sal said, Art through cuisine. I like the message. Phim had already helped himself to two portions. Ess gezunterheit, said Oriel. Beteavon, said the chef. Sahtain, said the other chef.

Inspired by Yolam Ottolenghi & Sami Tamimi cookbook Jerusalem.

Yaeli said, Here's a puzzle. The spoon and the fork got married. Who was the spoon and who was the fork? Sal laughed. Are you giving us the new version or the old? What about the knife, asked Phim. Ah, we're getting serious, said Ange. Irma said, I know who the spoon is. The question is whether the fork has legs or not. Joseph said, Obviously they had hands and feet but did they use them properly? Yaeli said, As long as they washed their hands. In India, said Oriel, they use fingers, and who's to say that's bad?

Phim said, I've always found circumcision difficult. Yaeli said, It's so deep for us. Something that happened to us when we were small, which we cannot remember, but bear the mark of it, and share the mark, upon all the males of our nation, setting us apart forever from all other peoples. Bound by blood spilt to God, it's the performing of the sacrifice upon the newly born males that is so important. Intense emotions are felt by mother and father. My baby boy be loved by God, and be protected by Him all your life – it is holy dedication.

Quietly patiently the quill scratched the parchment. It formed the aleph. We are not allowed to do this from memory, said the scribe, we have to look at the text. We have to speak the words. We are called soferim, synonymous with wisemen.   Phim said, What a noble tradition you continue.   Oriel said, The forming of letters is the growth of our mind.   Joseph said, I feel the Holy Spirit in this gift.   Sal said, Was it speech that made us truly human, or was it the writing down of speech in beautiful script, and listening and reading?

Chatting in the café. Can we discuss
the Messiah, asked Phim. Yaeli said,
You can't touch it. It's sacred to the
Jews; sacred to the Christians; Islam
refers to it. It's what we disagree about.
But I'll tell you a secret. No, I better not.
Do we want to ruin the life of faith, a
journey of growth and learning? Oriel
said, As we know deeper and higher, we
understand what they didn't tell us.
Enmity is the foe. Love is the truth.
When we know more fully, both Jew and
Christian and Muslim, we find truth in
the Messiah.

Friday afternoon. Join us for Sabbath
Dinner. They'd met outside the Hurva.
He was tall. Levi jeans, a light-blue
jacket. Yaeli bought a bottle of kosher
red (from Galilee). Shimon said the
kiddush (blessing over the wine). They
washed hands and sat around the table.
It'd been dressed with a white lace cloth
and silver cups. A piece of challah
(festive bread) dipped in salt. Phim said,
This is wonderful. Tell us what these are
called.   Pulkeh (chicken drumsticks),
matzah (unleavened bread), cholent a
traditional stew. I'm Ashkenazi from
Poland but my wife's family were in
Spain and Morocco (Sephardi).

Shimon said, Differences between
Ashkenazi and Sephardi? We lived and
grew in different worlds, and developed
different ways. Yiddish and Ladino.
Europe and Islam. Golden years in
Spain. Listen to this, he said, and
slipped a CD into the player. A Ladino
romancero (a sung narrative poem). It's
a rich tradition. A soprano sang
unaccompanied. A woman wept as she
washed the clothes. A knight passed by.
He'd been away at war. Give me a
drink, he said. She was gathering
water. You are my wife. I am not.
He told her the birth-mark, her secret
sign. It was him.

They divided into two groups at the entrance to King David's tomb. The guide said, This is open for constant prayers, 24 hours a day. It was maintained by Orthodox Jews, wearing black hats, and calling out prayers in Yiddish. There was a small fore-chamber with pews, and an inner sanctuary. Tourists were allowed into the sanctuary. A rabbi stood there by the covered tomb singing out prayers. Yaeli said, It's Psalm 150. He raised his hands high. He leapt up and down. He got out a shofar and blew a shrill blast. No falling asleep here, thought Phim.

Inspired by YouTube posted by Zahi Shaked.

Is this the closest we get? asked Phim.
Pure rectangular lines. It was designed
to recall Solomon's Temple.   Sponsored
by Isaac Wolfson, inaugurated 1982,
read Phim.   Yaeli asked permission to
stand quietly and listen to the cantor.
They said No.   Phim explained their
purpose and looked the Rabbi in the eye.
They talked about the task. He smiled.
The women with the women.   It was an
imposing grand space. Four columnar
chandeliers were towers of light.   That
window is awesome, said Oriel.   It was
a discomforting swirl of colors. Red,
blue-green, purple.   Wake up, said
Yaeli.

The Rabbi, whose name was Chaim, stood with Phim.   This is "Ein Kitzvah," sung on holiday celebrations. Maybe you'll recognize some of the words: Shimcha is Name; kodesh is holy. To summarize, There's no limit on you, O God. Sanctify thy name through us and through this Holy Sanctuary. The cantor and choir began.   It was a gathering-together of a tribe of trumpets, each outdoing the other, who would shout most joyfully, who could sound most highly. Speak aloud the blessings of His Holy Name.   Ha Ha they sang Pa Pa.   Pa Pa! said Phim, Ha Ha!

Sound of gunfire. An extremist faction was trying to topple the government. They were opposed to the liberal reforms. No recognition for Islam. Cancel the tax assisting the Arab-Jews. Bulldoze the Mosques. Israel under threat was the cry. Bullets smacked the wall of the street as they ran into an alley. A crazed man, eyes dark with anger, stood in their way, pointing a small machine gun. He started firing. No time to think, Sal stood in front of Phim, and took a couple of bullets. Ange crouching low sprinted forward and with full-force threw the man to the ground.

Sal lay in a pool of blood. Phim knelt beside him. Irma, help stop the bleeding. Two bullets. One in the upper left chest. The other through the flesh of his arm. Sal groaned. I've been lucky. Stop the bleeding. Hospital. He fainted, growing pale. The bullet had gone through leaving a large wound. Yaeli was already phoning friends. Phim, overwhelmed at the possibility of losing Sal, cried out, Fight, Sal, Fight! We've got work to do. I can't lose you! Sal was unconscious. Irma said, Quiet, Phim. Push on this. Staunch the bleeding.

Profile

Stean Anthony

I'm British, based in Japan. I've written a series of books of poetry promoting understanding and peace. Find out more from the list at the end of this book. I have also published *Eco-Friendly Japan*, Eihosha, Tokyo (2008). *Monday Songs 1-7*, and *Eitanka 1* (pdf file textbook freely available on website – and sound files). Thanks to Yamaguchi MK for kind help.

New Projects

Japan Angels 2 (little verses)
Saint Mary 365 book 8 (verses dedicated to St Mary)
Samāwātiwal'ard (Book 4 in Phim's story)
Hana 2 (verses on the theme of flowers and other things)
Hagios Paulos 4 (verses on the theme of Saint Paul)
Heiankyō 2 (translations of classic Japanese poetry)
Sport 2 (verses on the theme of sport)

Author's profits from this publication to be divided equally between the following institutions. The principal Jewish Synagogue (United Synagogue and Bevis Marks) and Muslim Mosque in London (London Central Mosque and East London Mosque), the Patriarchal Stavropegic Monastery of St John the Baptist in Tolleshunt Knights, the Coptic Christian Center in Stevenage, and the National Shrine of Our Lady of Walsingham, Norfolk, England.

Stean Anthony Books with Yamaguchi Shoten. Original poetry & translations & adaptations. Most are textbooks.

- *Selections from Shakespeare 1-5* (selected passages)
- *Great China 1-4* (transl. of classical Chinese poetry)
- *Kŏngzĭ 136* (poems based on the sayings of Confucius)
- *Manyōshū 365* (transl. of ancient Japanese poems)
- *One Hundred Poems* (poems based on the Japanese classical anthology 百人一首 *Hyakunin Isshu*)
- *Heiankyō 1* (translations of ancient Japanese poems)
- *Inorijuzu* (Buddhist & Christian words for peace)
- *Soulsongs* (poems for peace in Jerusalem)
- *Sufisongs* (poems for peace in Jerusalem)
- *Pashsongs* (songs & poems by Stean Anthony)
- *Bird* (poems on the theme of birds)
- *Sport* (poems on the theme of sport)
- *Hana 1* (poems on the theme of flowers)
- *Japan Angels 1* (little poems on the theme of angels)

- *Songs 365* (poems based on the Psalms)
- *Songs 365* (in Japanese poems based on the Psalms)
- *Songs for Islam* (poems based on verses in the Koran)
- *Isaiah Isaiah Bright Voice* (poems inspired by *Isaiah*)
- *Saint Paul 200* (poetic phrases from St Paul)
- *Hagios Paulos 1-3* (poetry based on the life of St Paul)

- *Gospel 365* (based on the Synoptic Gospels)
- *Saint John 550* (poetic version of *St John*)
- *Saint John 391* (verses in Japanese from the Gospel)
- *Saint John 190* (verses Japanese from Catholic Letters)
- *Saint Matthew 331* (songs Japanese from the Gospel)
- *Saint Mary 100* (poems dedicated to St Mary)
- *Saint Mary 365 Book 1-7* (calendar of poems themes relating to Mary, flowers, icons, prayers, scripture)
- *Saint Luke 132* (verses in Japanese from the Gospel)
- *Saint Mark 454* (verses in Japanese from the Gospel)

- *Messages to My Mother 1-7* (essays on faith etc)
- *Mozzicone 1-2* (essays on faith etc)
- *Monday Songs 1-7* (pdf textbooks of English songs)
- *Eitanka 1* (pdf textbook teaching poetry)
- *Psalms in English* (70 lectures in English teaching the Psalms pdf textbook)

- *Exnihil* (Book 1 in Phim's story)
- *Bərešitbara* (Book 2 in Phim's story)
- *Enarchae* (Book 3 in Phim's story)

ENARCHAE
by Stean Anthony

Company：Yamaguchi Shoten
Address：4-2 Kamihate-cho, Kitashirakawa
　　　　　Sakyo-ku, Kyoto, 606-8252
　　　　　Japan
Tel. 075-781-6121
Fax. 075-705-2003

ENARCHAE　　　　定価 2,000円（本体1,818円＋税）

2021年3月20日 初 版

著　者　Stean　Anthony
発行者　山 口 ケ イ コ
印刷所　大村印刷株式会社
発行所　株式会社　山口書店
〒606-8252京都市左京区北白川上終町4-2
TEL：075-781-6121　FAX：075-705-2003

ISBN 978-4-8411-7010-8　C1182